W9-BUE-689

NEIL T. ANDERSON
VICTORY
OVER THE
DARKNESS
STUDY GUIDE
REALIZING THE POWER OF YOUR IDENTITY IN CHRIST

LISA GUEST, EDITOR

Regal

A Division of Gospel Light
Ventura, California, U.S.A.

Published by Regal Books
A Division of Gospel Light
Ventura, California, U.S.A.
Printed in U.S.A.

Regal Books is a ministry of Gospel Light, an evangelical Christian publisher dedicated to serving the local church. We believe God's vision for Gospel Light is to provide church leaders with biblical, user-friendly materials that will help them evangelize, disciple and minister to children, youth and families.

It is our prayer that this Regal Book will help you discover biblical truth for your own life and help you meet the needs of others. May God richly bless you.

For a free catalog of resources from Regal Books/Gospel Light please contact your Christian supplier or call 1-800-4-GOSPEL.

Rights for publishing this book in other languages are contracted by Gospel Literature International (GLINT). GLINT also provides technical help for the adaptation, translation and publishing of Bible study resources and books in scores of languages worldwide. For further information, contact GLINT, P.O. Box 4060, Ontario, CA 91761-1003, U.S.A., or the publisher.

Contents

A NOTE FROM NEIL ANDERSON

Luke 5:1-11 is my favorite account of how the Lord taught. Jesus was instructing the multitudes from Peter's boat. "And when He had finished speaking, He said to Simon, 'Put out into the deep water and let down your nets for a catch'" (v. 4). Jesus had stopped talking but He had not stopped teaching. Peter heard what Jesus said, but he hadn't learned until he got into the boat and put out the nets.

This study guide gives you an opportunity to get into the boat and put out the nets. You can do it alone, but I recommend that you do it with other faithful learners. It provides an opportunity for more collective wisdom, and greater learning always takes place in the context of committed relationships. Developing trusting relationships and being devoted to one another in prayer is what makes group study so enriching.

I am thankful for the tremendous work that Lisa Guest, who also developed the study guide for *The Bondage Breaker* (Harvest House, 1990), has done in putting together this study guide. Another helpful resource is *Breaking Through to Spiritual Maturity* (Gospel Light, 1992), a curriculum for teaching these truths in a Sunday School class or small group. Since all this material has been professionally videotaped, you may want to consider an hour of video instruction each week and then use this study guide for group interaction. A summary of resources available from Freedom in Christ Ministries is given at the end of this study guide.

It is my prayer that you will fully realize who you are in Christ and learn to live as a child of God. If this study guide helps make that possible, I will be thankful. May the grace and love of our heavenly Father bless you with all the riches of your inheritance in Christ.

Neil T. Anderson

Who Are You?

J ESUS PROMISES HIS PEOPLE THAT "You shall know the truth, and the truth shall make you free" (John 8:32). Our identity in Jesus Christ is a fundamental truth that we believers need to understand, if we are to experience this promised freedom and grow to Christian maturity.

DATE: _____

WHO ARE YOU?

(PAGES 17-18)

"Who are you?" It sounds like a simple question, but attempting to answer it soon reveals the complexity of the issue. How would you answer the question if someone asked you, "Who are you?"?

We tend to identify ourselves and each other by what we look like, what we do, and perhaps even our theological position, our denominational preference, or our role in the church. But is who you are determined by what you do, look like and believe in? Or, is what you do, look like and believe in determined by who you are? That's an important question, especially as it relates to Christian maturity.

• Neil Anderson believes that your hope for growth, meaning and fulfillment as a Christian is based on understanding who you are, specifically your identity in Christ as a child of God. Your understanding of who you are is the critical foundation for your belief structure and your behavior patterns as a Christian.

Do you naturally identify yourself as a child of God as you think about who you are? Why or why not?

_____

_____

_____

Where in your own life do you see a connection between your belief structure and your behavior patterns? Give an example or two of how your beliefs about yourself influence your behavior.

_____

_____

_____

What changes in your behavior might result if you were able to clearly see yourself as the much-loved child of God that you are?

_____

_____

_____

DATE: _____

FALSE EQUATIONS IN THE SEARCH FOR IDENTITY

(PAGES 18-22)

• Neil tells of an attractive 17-year-old girl who, from the outside, seemed to have everything going for her: excellent grades, musical talent, a full-ride university scholarship, a wonderful wardrobe and a brand-new car.

What does your appearance suggest about you? What do you think people see as they look at you?

_____

_____

_____

_____

• Upon talking with Mary, Neil quickly realized that what was on the inside didn't match the outside. He asked Mary, "Have you ever cried yourself to sleep at night because you felt inadequate and wished you were somebody else?" Through her tears, she answered, "Yes."

Perhaps, like Mary, you have felt inadequate and wished you were somebody else. How does what is inside you differ from your outward appearance? Comment on any discrepancy between the outward appearance and the inner reality.

_____

_____

_____

Shame, fear, insecurity, loneliness, past hurts—there are many reasons why people, intentionally or otherwise, hide their real self from others. Why do you hide your real self under an outside appearance that is so different from what is inside?

_____

_____

_____

• Often what we show on the outside is a false front arising from our belief that if we appear attractive, perform well or enjoy a certain amount of status, then we will have it all together inside as well. But such is not the case. You plus attractiveness, you plus good performance and you plus status do not equal wholeness and significance. The only identity equation that works in God's kingdom is you plus Christ. Only you plus Christ equals wholeness and meaning.

How did you learn that being attractive, performing well or earning status does not mean wholeness or win you love?

_____

_____

_____

In what area(s) of your life has Christ given you the wholeness and meaning you once were seeking?

_____

_____

In what area(s) of your life would you like Jesus to give you wholeness and meaning?

_____

_____

_____

In God's kingdom, everyone has the same opportunity for a meaningful life. Why? Because wholeness and meaning in life are not products of what you have or don't have, what you've done or haven't done. In Christ you are already a whole person positionally and you already possess a life of infinite meaning and purpose because of who you are—a child of God.

• Although a Christian's identity in Christ is the key to wholeness, many believers have difficulty with self-worth, spiritual growth and maturity. One reason is that believers have been deceived by the devil. This great deceiver has distorted our true identity in Christ.

What false ideas, which are results of the work of the great deceiver, may you have about who you are?

_____

_____

_____

Asking a person about false ideas about him- or herself may be like asking fish about the water they swim in. The individual can't see what is so much a part of his or her reality. If you're not sure which ideas about yourself are false, ask someone you trust to help you see yourself as God sees you. Also, spend some time in prayer asking God to help you see yourself through His eyes.

_____

_____

_____

• Neil tells of a person convinced that she was evil. While she may have done some evil things, she wasn't evil. She did, however, let Satan's accusations about her behavior influence her perception of her identity instead of letting her identity—as a child of God in Christ—influence her behavior.

In what ways are you caught in this same trap? Have you, for instance, failed at something and therefore see yourself as a failure? Are you basing your identity on something you've done rather than on who you are in Christ? Be specific, and then, as you pray about this entrapment, thank God that He sees you as His child.

_____

_____

_____

Why would it be to your disadvantage to focus on the missteps you've taken in your life?

_____

_____

_____

When we swallow Satan's lie and believe that what we do makes us what we are, that false belief sends us into a tailspin of hopelessness and defeat.

DATE: _____

OUR POSITIVE INHERITANCE FROM CREATION

(PAGES 22-29)

Genesis 1 and 2 tell how God created Adam and Eve in His image and make it clear that, besides the physical life that we inherited from Adam, we also inherited the capacity for spiritual life (see Gen. 1:26,27). For the Christian, to be spiritually alive is to be in union with God by being in Christ. And that union with God means three important things for believers.

Significance—The dominion that Adam exercised before the Fall has been restored to you as a Christian. As a child of God, you have important work to do for your Lord. Also, as part of your inheritance in Christ, Satan has no authority over you.

Safety and Security—Adam was completely cared for in the garden. Likewise, we who follow Christ lack nothing. Safety and security are another facet of our inheritance in Christ.

Belonging—A true sense of belonging comes not only from knowing that we belong to God, but also from belonging to each other.

• **Significance, Safety and Security, and Belonging**

Which of these is most appealing to you right now? Why?

_____

_____

_____

Which of these seems most unreachable to you? Why?

_____

_____

_____

Significance, safety and security, and belonging—these were no longer attributes once sin entered the world.

DATE: _____

OUR NEGATIVE INHERITANCE FROM THE FALL
(PAGES 29-36)

The effects of man's fall were dramatic, immediate and far-reaching, infecting every subsequent member of the human race; infecting you. We'll look at five aspects of our negative inheritance from the Fall.

• **Spiritual Death**—With the Fall, Adam and Eve's union with God was severed. They were separated from God.

When did you first become aware of your separation from God? What circumstances brought you to the realization that you needed God?

_____

_____

_____

Maybe you're just now realizing your need for God. In a brief prayer, tell Him of your need and how you have fallen short of being the person He wants you to be. Read 1 John 1:9 and thank God for the gift of His forgiveness. Cleansed and forgiven because of Jesus' death on your behalf, accept Jesus as your Savior and ask Him to help you live with Him as Lord of your life. (It is important to find a church body that will help you grow in your knowledge of and commitment to God.)

_____

_____

_____

• **Lost Knowledge of God**—The Fall affected the way Adam and Eve (and you and I) think. The fact that Adam and Eve tried to hide from God (see Gen. 3:7,9) clearly indicates a faulty understanding of who God is.

When have you tried to hide from God? What prompted that attempt?

_____

_____

_____

Are you trying to hide from God right now? If so, what is causing you to do this? Read Psalm 23. Hear God's words of love for you. Believe the truth that you have no reason to hide from a loving and forgiving God.

_____

_____

_____

• In God's original design, knowledge was relational. Adam and Eve knew God by being with God. When they lost their relationship with God, they lost the knowledge of God that was intrinsic to that relationship. In our unregenerate state, we know something about God, but we don't know God because we have a broken relationship with Him. When we enter God's family, however, we can know God as Adam and Eve did.

Describe the differences in your life once you took the step from knowing *about* God to *knowing* Him. How is the "after" picture different from the "before" picture? How are you a different person now that you know God personally?

_____

_____

In Christ we are able to know God personally. Our relationship with God through Christ is the cornerstone of our identity.

• **Dominant Negative Emotions**—Not only did the Fall affect mankind's thinking, it also affected us emotionally.

> For one thing, we became fearful and anxious. What fears dominated your life before you realized that you are a child of God? (The fact that these fears may continue to intrude doesn't make you less of a Christian.)

> _____

> _____

> _____

> Another emotional by-product of sin is shame and guilt. What have been some sources of shame and guilt in your life?

> _____

> _____

> _____

> Mankind also became depressed and angry after the Fall. What events and circumstances trigger your feelings of depression and/or anger?

> _____

> _____

> Fear and anxiety, shame and guilt, depression and anger. What would God have you do with these powerful and destructive emotions?

> _____

> _____

> In Genesis 4, God talks to an angry Cain about his feelings and says, "If you do what is right, will you not be accepted?" (v. 7, *NIV*). In other words, if you do what is right, you won't feel angry and depressed. When have you noticed that bad feelings follow wrong behavior and/or good feelings follow right behavior? Be specific.

> _____

> _____

> _____

Think about your life right now. What changes in your actions need to be made in light of the truth about the relationship between feelings and behavior?

_____

_____

_____

• **Too Many Choices**—The Fall affected our will as well as our thinking and our emotions. In the garden, everything that Adam and Eve wanted to do was okay except eating from the tree of the knowledge of good and evil (see Gen. 2:16,17). One result of their bad choice to eat from that tree is the myriad of good and bad choices you and I face every day.

Which choices that you face bring into clearest focus the sharp contrast between your will and what God would have you do?

_____

_____

_____

What can you do to insure that your choices are the choices God would have you make?

_____

_____

_____

• **Attributes Become Needs**—Another long-term effect of sin is that man's glowing attributes before the Fall became glaring needs after the Fall. Acceptance was replaced by rejection, so we feel the need to belong.

When you have felt the need to be accepted by God and/or by people, what steps have you taken to meet that need?

_____

_____

_____

How has God met this need in your life? How can you help meet the needs of others?

_____

_____

• Innocence was replaced by guilt and shame, so we need our sense of worth restored.

> If you have a low sense of worth, if you are your harshest critic, or if you have a hard time liking yourself, what have you done (or what could you do) to overcome this?

> _____

> _____

> _____

> How is your identity in Christ—or, how might your identity in Christ be—the means to overcome a negative self-image?

> _____

> _____

> _____

• Authority was replaced by weakness and helplessness, so we strive for strength and self-control.

> How have you, during times of weakness and helplessness, found strength and peace in the Lord? Be specific about the circumstances.

> _____

> _____

> _____

> Neil Anderson observes that, "The human soul was not designed to function as a master. You'll either serve the true God or the god of this world." Consider how you spend your time, your talents and your money. Whom are you serving and, if you can figure it out, why?

> _____

> _____

> _____

• We human beings have several basic human needs. Since the Fall, we've had the need to belong, the need to have our sense of worth restored and the need to have strength and self-control.

> As Neil Anderson observes, sinful behavior is a wrong attempt to meet these basic needs. What evidence from your own life supports

this observation? In other words, when have your attempts to meet basic needs led you to sin? Know that, as one who calls Jesus "Lord," you are forgiven for the sins you confess (see 1 John 1:9).

_____

_____

_____

As God's unique creation, you have significance. As a child of God, you can find safety and security. As a member of God's family, you can experience a sense of belonging.

DATE: _____

LIVING WHAT YOU LEARN

Guided by the truths of this chapter, answer the question, "Who are you?" Through the week, use some of the answers to "who you are" to counter any negative thoughts you have about yourself.

_____

_____

A WORD OF PRAYER

Father God, it is a privilege to be Your child. It is a gift of grace I don't fully comprehend. I thank You for Your wondrous love for me and ask that You would help me lead a life that honors You. Help me live according to the truth that my identity is based on who I am in Christ. May I see myself through Your eyes. May I understand more clearly how much You love me and let that love empower and guide me. I pray in the name of Jesus Christ through whom You graciously demonstrated Your amazing love for sinful me, amen.

LOOKING AHEAD

As a believer, your true identity is not based on what you do or what you possess, but on who you are in Christ. You will better understand who you are in Christ when you see how Jesus won back for you the identity that was lost when man was expelled from the garden. Christ's triumph and what it has gained for you is the theme of the next chapter.

Forever Different

As we've seen, many Christians are not enjoying the maturity and freedom that is theirs in Christ because they hold wrong perceptions about themselves. They don't see themselves as they really are in Christ. They don't grasp their true identity. They identify themselves with the wrong Adam.

DATE: _____

A DRAMATIC CHANGE

(PAGES 37-39)

• Remember the story of Biff and the example of Eric Liddle?

What does the story of Biff say to you about the race you are running for the Lord, your focus and your fitness?

_____

_____

_____

Olympic runner Eric Liddle withdrew from a race scheduled on Sunday—a race he might have won—in honor of his heavenly Father. When has your commitment to the Lord caused you to take a stand that many people around you didn't understand?

_____

_____

_____

We Christians are salt and light in a dying and dark world because of the dramatic change that occurs in us the moment we trust in Jesus.

DATE: _____

THE LIFE-CHANGING DIFFERENCE OF THE LAST ADAM
(PAGES 39-41)

Too many Christians identify with the first Adam—with the Adam who sinned and was exiled from the presence of God. In reality, however, Christians are identified with Jesus Christ, the last Adam. As a result, the difference in your history is eternally profound. You need to be sure you're identifying with the right Adam, with Jesus your Savior.

• What we notice about Jesus is His complete dependence on God the Father.

> Where do you struggle and, like the first Adam, even fail to depend completely on God? What areas of your life (attitudes, responsibilities, etc.) are you reluctant to surrender to God?

_____

_____

_____

> What keeps you from trusting God and depending on Him completely? Confess those barriers that keep you from trusting and ask God to help your lack of faith (see Mark 9:24).

_____

_____

_____

> When have you taken a step of faith and found God faithful beyond your greatest expectations? Describe that experience in detail and let it serve as a touchstone the next time you need to step out in faith.

_____

_____

_____

Where do you have the opportunity to take a step of faith today? What might happen, best-and worst-case scenario, if you took that step? Share your concerns, fears and hopes with God and ask for His guidance and courage as you take the step.

_____

_____

_____

• Both Jesus and Adam were born spiritually alive. But Jesus, unlike Adam, *stayed* spiritually alive. Adam died spiritually when he sinned.

Where do you, like the first Adam, fall short of God's will for you? Confess areas of persistent sin in your life and ask God to help you find strength in Him when Satan attacks and offers temptations to which he knows you are especially susceptible.

_____

_____

_____

Now read Matthew 4:1-11. What does this scene from Jesus' life show you about how to resist sin?

_____

_____

_____

What specific step would you like to take this week to become better acquainted with God's Word so that, like Jesus, you can better resist sin? Start with a realistic goal such as reading a passage of Scripture each day, attending a Bible study, or taking your Bible to church so that you can follow the sermon more closely. Let reaching this goal be the first step toward wielding the sword of the Spirit when Satan attacks (see Eph. 6:17).

_____

_____

What difference does it make to a Christian—to you and me—that Jesus was 100 percent dependent on God and that He did not forfeit His spiritual life by sinning? It's the difference between life and death.

DATE: _____

WHAT A DIFFERENCE CHRIST'S DIFFERENCE MAKES IN US!

(PAGES 41-45)

• In 1 Corinthians 15:22, Paul writes, "As in Adam all die, so also in Christ all shall be made alive."

What does the phrase "in Christ" mean to you personally as you live out your life day by day?

_____

_____

• New life in Christ begins when you first trust Jesus as your Lord and Savior, and that new life means a new identity. In turn, that new identity means a new way of living as you live out who you are as a child of God.

How does (or how would) seeing yourself as a much-loved child of God enable you to better live the Christian life?

_____

_____

Satan can do nothing to damage your position and identity in Christ, but if he can deceive you into believing that you are not acceptable to God and that you'll never amount to anything as a Christian, then you will live according to those debilitating thoughts rather than in the freedom and wholeness available to you in Christ. What thoughts about yourself may be deceptions generated by Satan?

_____

_____

God calls you a saint, and that glorious truth should overshadow the lies about yourself that Satan would have you believe. What truths about your identity in Christ can you use to counter Satan's deceptions about who you are? (If you're not sure, keep working through this lesson!)

_____

_____

Often we have to act as if we love someone before we find ourselves loving that person. That principle of acting first and letting feelings follow may need to function in your life if you are to live out your identity in Christ. So what can you do today to live like a saint, like a person loved and called by God, rather than a sinner, a person hunched over by a sense of unworthiness and failure?

_____

_____

_____

Remember that what you do doesn't determine who you are (for instance, failing at something doesn't make you a failure). Rather, who you are (a child of God) determines what you do if you let yourself believe the truth that God loves you. After all, you can't consistently behave in a way that's inconsistent with the way you perceive yourself.

DATE:_____

WHAT IS TRUE OF CHRIST IS TRUE OF YOU
(PAGES 45-49)

One way to perceive yourself as God does is to reaffirm who you are in Christ.

• In the *Victory over the Darkness* text, you were invited to read aloud the list of answers to the question "Who Am I?" found on pages 45-47. Whether or not you accepted that invitation then, do so now. Read slowly the list of answers. Let yourself hear the words and be amazed by God's grace to you.

If you hesitate to read aloud these wonderful words of God's love, what are your reasons?

_____

_____

Which statements of fact are especially meaningful to you right now?

_____

_____

Why do these two or three truths you just listed mean so much to you?

_____

_____

_____

How would believing the truths you listed above make your life different?

_____

_____

You can make the truths you listed more meaningful and productive in your life by simply choosing to believe what God has said about you. That sounds simple enough, but why isn't that step easy for you to take?

_____

_____

Lay before God your answer to the previous question. Ask God to heal those places where you've been hurt, to strengthen you where you've been crippled and to free you where you have been in chains and unable to know His love for you.

_____

_____

_____

One of the greatest ways to help yourself grow into maturity in Christ is to continually remind yourself who you are in Him. The more you reaffirm who you are in Christ, the more your behavior will begin to reflect your true identity.

DATE: _____

THE BRIGHT HOPE OF BEING A CHILD OF GOD

(PAGES 49-50)

If you're beginning to think you are someone special as a Christian, you're right! You are special not because of anything you've done but because of God's gracious invitation to be His child.

• Read again the words of 1 John 3:1-3 and hear the wonder in the apostle's voice.

What hope for today do you find in these verses?

_____

_____

_____

What hope for the future do you find in 1 John 3:1-3?

_____

_____

_____

The hope you as a believer have in God is a present hope as well as a future hope. Someday you will be changed into Christ's image, but you are a child of God now and you can live according to this truth.

DATE: _____

LIVING WHAT YOU LEARN

On some 3x5-inch cards, write out the most meaningful answers to the question "Who Am I?" (one per card) and pray through those truths each day this week. Ask God to help you believe these words—words He has spoken *about* you and *to* you so that you may experience freedom and wholeness in Him.

A WORD OF PRAYER

Father in heaven, what a privilege to address You as such! I

marvel that You name me Your child and I ask that You

would help me believe who I am. Help me to believe who I

am in Christ that I may better live out the Christian life as

Your witness and as a vessel of Your love and grace. And,
Lord God, keep me focused on the race I have to run as Your
child. Give me boldness to take a stand for You, unafraid of
being different from the people, the culture, the society
around me. May I, Almighty and All-Loving God, depend,
like Jesus, completely on You. In His name I pray, amen.

LOOKING AHEAD

If you take nothing else away from this lesson, take this truth: You cannot
consistently live in a manner that is inconsistent with how you perceive
yourself. You must see yourself as a child of God in order to live like a
child of God.

See Yourself for Who You Really Are

Y OU ARE A CHILD OF GOD, and that fact has bearing on your present life now as well as on your eternal life. Consider how that fact can affect your life now.

DATE:_____

SEE YOURSELF FOR WHO YOU REALLY ARE

(PAGES 51-53)

• Reconsider the stories of Claire and Derek.

As a college student, Claire simply believed what she perceived herself to be (a child of God) and so was committed to being transformed into His image and to loving people. How did you react to the description of Claire when you first read it in the *Victory over the Darkness* text? What aspect of Claire's journey revealed an important truth to you?

_____

_____

_____

_____

Derek was well into his 30s before he learned that God is not a perfectionistic, impossible-to-please heavenly Father. He also realized that he already was pleasing God by who he is in Christ. How did you react to Derek's story? What aspect of Derek's journey revealed an important truth to you?

_____

_____

With whom do you identify most closely: Claire who is confident about her identity in the Lord or Derek who had to learn the truth about his heavenly Father? Comment on the similarity you've noted.

_____

_____

DATE: _____

THEOLOGY BEFORE PRACTICALITY
(PAGES 53-60)

The experiences of Claire and Derek illustrate the importance of establishing our Christian lives on right beliefs about God and ourselves. We need to understand who we are as a result of who God is and what He has done (i.e., theology) before we can live out our faith (i.e., practical Christianity).

• Many Christians struggle to live out their faith because they try to base their spiritual growth and maturity on practical sections of the Scriptures (what we need to do to live out our faith) and spend too little time internalizing the doctrinal sections (what we need to know about God, ourselves, sin and salvation).

Consider your own Bible reading patterns. What do you tend to focus on? Why?

_____

_____

In light of what you've read so far in *Victory over the Darkness*, what value would internalizing doctrinal sections of Scripture have for someone struggling with the question "Who am I?"?

_____

_____

• When you don't understand the biblical truths pertaining to your position in Christ, you have no ground for success in the practical arena. How can you hope, for instance, to "stand firm against the schemes of the devil" (Eph. 6:11) if you have not internalized the truth that you are already victoriously "raised...up with Him, and seated...with Him in the heavenly places, in Christ Jesus" (Eph. 2:6)? How can you rejoice in hope and persevere in tribulation (see Rom. 12:12) without the confidence of knowing you have been justified by faith and have peace with God through the Lord Jesus Christ (see Rom. 5:1)?

> When has God's truth served you well in the practical arena? Perhaps the truth that you are already victorious over Satan through Christ (see Eph. 2:6) has helped you stand strong against his temptations. Also, perhaps knowing that you have been justified by faith through Jesus (see Rom. 5:1) has helped you persevere in difficult times. Describe in detail such a time.

> In what area(s) of your life are you struggling to live out your faith right now? Outline the situation and then spend some time with your Bible. Find a doctrinal truth that can help you live out your faith in the circumstances you just described.

When your basic belief system about God and yourself is shaky, your day-to-day behavior system will be shaky. But, as experiences from your own life may have reminded you, when your belief system is intact and your relationship with God is based on truth, you'll have very little trouble working out the practical aspects of daily Christianity.

• The music director and his wife whose marriage was failing found that, when each of them got right with God, they were able to work out their problems. Getting right with each other began with getting right with God. But what does "getting right with God" mean? Getting right with God always begins with settling once and for all the issue that God is your loving Father and you are His accepted child.

Why would wholehearted acceptance of this truth help two individuals through the problems of their marriage?

_____

_____

What problems would be alleviated by your wholehearted acceptance of the truth that God loves you?

_____

_____

• As long as you believe that God is your loving Father and you are His accepted child, your faith will permeate your daily experience. If you don't accept that truth, you will struggle to earn the acceptance that is already yours in Christ.

When have you tried to earn God's acceptance? What did you do?

_____

_____

What lesson did you learn from the experience?

_____

_____

• Hear these freeing words: We don't serve God to gain His acceptance; we are accepted, so we serve God. We don't follow Him in order to be loved; we are loved, so we follow Him.

What tends to motivate your worship and your service?

_____

_____

Think about your relationship to your spouse, a favorite family member or a special friend. What is it about the relationship that frees you to give and receive?

_____

_____

_____

See Yourself
for Who You
Really Are

Thank God for placing people in your life who accept you as you are, thus helping you learn about His gracious and unconditional love.

_____

_____

Satan will try to convince you that you are an unworthy, unacceptable, sin-sick person who will never amount to anything in God's eyes. But that isn't who you are, and believing Satan's lie will lock you into a defeated, fruitless life. Contrary to what Satan would have you believe, you are a saint (Eph. 1:1) whom God has declared righteous, and believing this truth about your identity will set you free.

• As you read in the previous chapter, one way to learn to perceive yourself as God does is to reaffirm who you are in Christ. The "Who Am I?" list was designed to help you do just that. Here in chapter 3 you find a supplement to the list of answers to that question.

In the *Victory over the Darkness* text, you were invited to read aloud the truths listed on pages 57-58. Whether or not you accepted the invitation then, consider doing so now. Read slowly the list of statements that describes your identity in Christ, and do this regularly until these truths become a part of you.

Which statements are especially meaningful to you right now?

_____

_____

Why do you think the truths you just listed mean so much?

_____

_____

If you could believe the truths you listed above, how would your life be different?

_____

_____

_____

Ask God to help these truths about the effects of God's grace enter your heart and not just your mind. Also, as before, ask Him to heal those places where you've been hurt, to strengthen you where you've been crippled and to free you where you have been in chains and unable to know His love for you.

_____

_____

Your perception of your identity makes a big difference in how well you live out your faith and deal with the challenges and conflicts of life. And the only basis for an accurate identity is God's unfailing Word.

DATE: _____

THERE'S A DIFFERENCE BETWEEN RELATIONSHIP AND FELLOWSHIP
(PAGES 60-62)

Perhaps this emphasis on God's complete acceptance of you in Christ has raised the question "What happens to this relationship when I sin?" The grace-filled answer is that there is nothing you can do to change the fact that you are related to Father God by spiritual birth. Your relationship with God was forever settled when you were born into His family.

• Just as you will always be related to your biological father and mother, you will always be related to your spiritual Father. And just as you lived in harmony with your father when you obeyed him, you will live in harmony with your heavenly Father when you obey Him. (You might consult your church's or pastor's views on this point.)

Consider a time of disobedience and disharmony with God. What did you learn from that experience?

_____

_____

Have you ever worried that you had forfeited your relationship with your heavenly Father? If not, why not? If so, what reassurance did you find that, even in your sinfulness, you hadn't forfeited your status as His child? If you are worried right now, review the truths of John 10:27,28; Romans 8:35,39; and 1 Peter 1:18,19.

_____

_____

Right now are you living in harmony with your heavenly Father or taking advantage of your gracious relationship with your heavenly Father? Explain why you answer as you do.

_____

_____

What can you do to enrich your fellowship with your heavenly Father?

_____

_____

Think about your life right now. What decision or situation, if any, becomes clear in light of this call to obey God?

_____

_____

Know that there is nothing you can do to improve upon your relationship with God other than believing that it is true. You are a child of God, period. The only thing you can do to improve the harmony of your relationship with God is to believe the truth and live in submissive obedience to Him.

DATE: _____

BELIEVE WHAT YOU PERCEIVE IN OTHERS

(PAGES 62-64)

• As important as it is that you believe in your true identity as a child of God, it is equally important that you perceive other Christians as children of God as well and treat them accordingly.

The statistics are frightening: for every positive statement a child hears, he or she receives 10 negative statements. What kinds of statements are the children in your life hearing from you? Let your answer prompt a minute or two of prayer.

_____

_____

_____

What kinds of statements are fellow Christians in your life hearing from you? Again, let your answer prompt a minute or two of prayer.

_____

_____

Who in your life has been a vessel of God's grace with his or her words of edification and encouragement? Thank God for that person, and perhaps thank that person in a note or with a phone call!

_____

_____

DATE: _____

BELIEVING WHAT YOU PERCEIVE

(PAGES 64-67)

• Remember the story of Jenny? When she began to walk by faith, seeing herself for who she really is in Christ, her behavior began to conform to the truth about her spiritual identity.

Look at yourself as objectively as possible. Where does your behavior not match your Christian beliefs?

_____

_____

What is at the root of this inconsistency? Failure to obey God's commands? Failure to believe who you are in Him? Both? Other factors?

_____

_____

_____

What will you do to bring your behavior in line with your faith? And who will you choose to help you make the change, to enable you to see yourself as God's child and to hold you accountable on your journey toward spiritual maturity?

_____

_____

See yourself as God's child. Read the truths about yourself listed in chapters 3 and 4; believe them and walk in them. When you do, your behavior as a Christian will conform to what you believe as you walk by faith.

DATE: _____

LIVING WHAT YOU LEARN

What is one thing you can do this week to bring more harmony to your relationship with your heavenly Father? Consider persistent or habitual sins that He can help you resist (see 1 Cor. 10:13).

_____

_____

_____

Who is one person you can ask God to help you see through His eyes so that you can offer him or her words of grace rather than thoughts of criticism, dislike or anger? Pray and then consider extending an act of grace, trusting that your feelings will follow.

_____

_____

_____

A WORD OF PRAYER

God of grace, I thank You that my ability to serve You is not what gains Your acceptance, that my ability to follow You is not what determines whether I am loved. Thank You for Your acceptance that frees me to serve You and Your love that frees me to follow You. And I thank You for the security of my relationship with You. May I believe that truth and base my life on it. Help me, Lord, to be obedient so that my relationship with You may be harmonious. And, God, so that there is greater harmony within Your Body, help me see Your people through Your eyes. And help me control my tongue so that I speak only words that build up, not words that hurt and tear down. I pray in Jesus' name and for His sake, amen.

LOOKING AHEAD

The Bible teaches that you are a child of God. Nevertheless you are still less than perfect in your behavior. You are a saint who sins, and that is the great Christian dilemma that the next chapter addresses.

CHAPTER FOUR

Something Old, Something New

THE GREAT CHRISTIAN TRUTH IS THAT, IN CHRIST, you are declared righteous and are completely acceptable to God. The great Christian dilemma is that, despite this gracious provision, we Christians are still less than perfect in our behavior. While our position in Christ is solid, our daily performance is often marked by failure and disobedience.

DATE:_____

SOMETHING OLD, SOMETHING NEW

(PAGES 69-70)

• In Romans 7, Paul groans, "The good that I wish, I do not do; but I practice the very evil that I do not wish" (v. 19).

> What is "the good" that you wish to do but somehow don't or can't manage to do?

_____

_____

_____

_____

What is "the very evil" that you do not wish to do but somehow don't or can't avoid?

_____

_____

If you can answer either of these two questions (and, if we're truthful, we all can answer both!), you know personally the struggle that believers have with their old patterns of behavior. A better understanding of this sinful side of your sainthood will help you see more clearly your identity in Christ and enable your further Christian growth.

DATE: _____

AM I THE ROPE IN A TUG-OF-WAR BETWEEN TWO NATURES?
(PAGE 70-75)

• To understand our new nature, we need to recognize the thoughts we have about ourselves.

Until now, what have you understood about the relationship between your old nature, your old self and sinful flesh, and your new nature as a child of God?

_____

_____

_____

What have been the consequences—emotional as well as behavioral—of your understanding about the relationship between your old nature and your new nature?

_____

_____

_____

Some believers think of two natures within them vying for control of their lives like two dogs intent on destroying one another. But if you believe that you are part light and part darkness, you will not live with the confidence, joy and freedom of a believer. Again, if Satan can get you to believe that you are fundamentally no different from a person who doesn't know Christ, then you will behave no differently from that person.

• Through God's work of atonement, through Christ's death on the cross for your sins, God changed sinners to saints. This inner change, this justification, occurred at the moment of your salvation. The outward change in your daily walk, the process of sanctification, continues throughout your life.

> Paul knew that he was "the foremost of sinners" before his conversion to Christ (see 1 Tim. 1:12-16), and he knew he was a very different person in Christ once he accepted Jesus as Lord and Savior (see 1 Cor. 15:9,10). Describe your life, your personality and your priorities before you accepted Jesus Christ as your Savior and Lord (the point of justification).
>
> _____
>
> _____
>
> _____
>
> What changes have occurred in you since accepting Jesus as your Savior and Lord that make the process of sanctification very evident to you? In what areas have you become more like the person God is calling and molding you to be?
>
> _____
>
> _____
>
> _____
>
> What aspect of your character, what facet of your life and/or what priorities would you like to see God work on next? Make this desire for sanctification the topic of a brief prayer.
>
> _____
>
> _____
>
> _____

Know that sanctification is only fully effective when the radical, inner transformation of justification is realized and appropriated by faith. That's one reason why it is so important to understand your identity in Christ.

• **The Nature of the Matter**—The New Testament teaches that when you came into spiritual union with God through your new birth, you didn't add a new, divine nature to your old, sinful nature. Instead, you exchanged natures.

Why is this fact a source of hope and encouragement?

_____

_____

_____

• A new Christian is like a lump of coal. With time and pressure, that coal becomes hardened and beautiful. The lump of coal consists of the right substance to become a diamond, and it does so.

Whom have you seen or known that was at first a lump of coal but, giving his or her life over to God, became a shining example and vessel of His love and grace? (Think about the apostle Paul if no one else comes to mind.) Describe what you saw of the process of that person's sanctification.

_____

_____

_____

Let that real-life example encourage you in your journey toward spiritual maturity, toward being a diamond-like light for your God.

• **Either One or the Other**—The Bible doesn't just teach that we were "in the dark" and we moved "into the light" at the point of salvation. The Bible also teaches that we "were darkness" and now we "are light" (Eph. 5:8).

Why is it significant that you weren't merely in the dark but that you were darkness and that you haven't simply moved into the light but that you are light?

_____

_____

_____

• Your new identity is already determined because the nature of Christ is within you, enabling you to be like Christ, not just act like Him. God knows that you can't solve the problem of your old sinful self by simply improving your behavior (acting like Christ). He knows He must change who you are and give you an entirely new self, made possible by the life of Christ in you.

What do these truths teach you about your heavenly Father? Praise Him for His wisdom and love!

_____

_____

_____

Only after God makes you a partaker of Christ's nature are you able to change your behavior. What behavior(s) have you seen change since becoming a Christian?

_____

_____

_____

• You are a spiritual person in Christ. That is your true identity. The issue now is learning to walk in harmony with who you really are.

Since becoming a Christian, when have you chosen to live according to the old way? Give an example or two.

_____

_____

_____

What were the consequences of your choice? Think about feeling or not feeling convicted, and describe any lessons you learned from that experience.

_____

_____

_____

The conviction that comes when we sin is another evidence of the presence of the nature of Christ within us. To sin is to violate our true nature as children of God.

DATE: _____

IS THE "OLD MAN" ALIVE, DYING OR ALREADY DEAD?

(PAGES 75-78)

• **Rest in Peace**—As the text explains, the death of your old self formally ended your relationship with sin, but it did not end sin's existence. Sin and Satan are still around, and they are strong and appealing.

> Stating clearly the points where you are particularly vulnerable to sin's enticements may help you stand strong against temptation. In what areas of your life are you especially likely to act independently of God and commit sin?

_____

_____

_____

> By virtue of the crucifixion of the old self, sin's power over you is broken (see Rom. 6:7,12,14). You are no longer under any obligation to serve sin, to obey sin or to respond to sin. Write a one- or two-line prayer based on this truth and use that prayer to help you stand strong in those areas of vulnerability you just identified.

_____

_____

_____

• **Once Dead, Always Dead**—Have you, like the pastor who visited Neil, been struggling because your old self hasn't died? Do you, like that pastor, need to be reminded that your old self died at the point of your salvation (see Col. 3:3)?

> Explain in your own words why you, and the pastor who visited Neil, don't need to be in turmoil over an old self that doesn't seem to have died yet.

_____

_____

_____

_____

What freedom for Christian joy and spiritual growth do you find in the truth of Colossians 3:3?

_____

_____

_____

Through the redemptive work of the Cross, your old self has died and been replaced by the life of Jesus Christ implanted in you. Believe it!

DATE: _____

WHERE DOES THE FLESH FIT INTO THE PICTURE?
(PAGES 78-85)

Just as Neil had to learn to react differently to the Navy ship's new skipper after two years under a tough old skipper, Christians who have the new life of Jesus Christ implanted within them have some adjusting to do.

• **Reacting to Your Old Skipper**—While your old skipper was in control, you developed a mind-set and lifestyle apart from God and centered on yourself. You learned to live your life independently of God, and your flesh—your thought patterns, memory traces, responses and habits—remains in opposition to God.

> Think about your actions, reactions, emotional responses, thought patterns, memories and habits. Name one or two that are still clearly in opposition to God and centered on yourself.

_____

_____

_____

> What does the Bible offer as an alternative to the behaviors and/or thoughts you just named? Ask God to help you live according to these models. Plan the first step you'll take, and take it!

_____

_____

_____

• **Responding to Your New Skipper**—Getting rid of the old self was God's responsibility, and He did so at the Cross. Now you are in Christ, and it is your responsibility to change your behavior. You may still choose wrongly to walk according to the flesh and your old desires.

To gain victory over the flesh, you must first learn to walk by the Spirit. What does it mean to you to "walk by the Spirit"? (That concept will become clearer in the next chapter.)

_____

_____

_____

Second, you must let your old patterns of thinking and responding be "transformed by the renewing of your mind" (see Rom. 12:2). What do you know about that process of transformation at this point? (Chapters 6-9 address this topic.)

_____

_____

_____

• What Role Does Sin Play in My Struggle Toward Saintly Behavior?—

We sin when we live independently of God, when we believe Satan's deception that meaning and purpose in life may be achieved apart from a personal relationship with, and obedience to, the Creator of life.

What circumstances in life helped you recognize Satan's deception and brought you to the point of naming Jesus as your Lord and Savior?

_____

_____

_____

When you received Christ, the power of sin was not broken, but its power to dominate you was. When have you found the strength in God that you needed to stand strong against the powerful appeal of sin? Be specific about the details and let this incident help you stand strong the next time you are tempted to sin.

_____

_____

_____

● **Doing What I Don't Want to Do**—Even the great apostle Paul struggled with doing what he didn't want to do. As he explains in Romans 7:17-21, the sin dwelling in him kept him from doing what he wanted to do.

Clearly, sin is not Paul or you. Sin is only dwelling in you, and you are responsible for not letting it reign. What aspect of this truth is new to you or, if not new, again reassuring?

_____

_____

_____

What freedom do you find in reading about Paul's struggle and about his conclusion in Romans 7:17-21?

_____

_____

_____

● **On the Battleground**—The desire to do right and the powerful appeal of sin battle each other in your mind.

Which of your thoughts give Satan a foothold?

_____

_____

What truths from Scripture can help you stand strong in this battle?

_____

_____

What do Romans 7:25 and 8:1 say about the battle you're waging?

_____

_____

The battle for your mind is a winnable war because, at the moment of your conversion, you became a new person in Christ. There is nothing you can do to improve upon the work of Christ in justifying you. You must choose to believe what He's done and accept your identity as His child.

DATE: _____

LIVING WHAT YOU LEARN

Focus on Romans 7:19: "The good that I wish, I do not do; but I practice the very evil that I do not wish." Make a list of "the good" that you would like to do and "the very evil" you would like to stop doing. List five or six items under each heading and then choose one of the good things to do today and an evil thing to stop doing, and then, with prayer, take action!

_____

_____

_____

A WORD OF PRAYER

Gracious God, thank You that my old self has died—and help me accept that truth on faith even though I continue to struggle with what my old self taught and conditioned me to think and do. Paul's words could easily be mine: "The good that I wish, I do not do; but I practice the very evil that I do not wish" (Rom. 7:19). I'm glad that You understand my struggle. By Your grace I choose to win the battle against sin and stand strong against its appeal. May I find real joy and freedom under my new Skipper. Teach me, Father God, to live so that the new life within—the life of Jesus Christ—can flourish. I pray in His precious name, amen.

LOOKING AHEAD

Sanctification is the process of becoming in your behavior what you already are in your identity. Spiritual growth and maturity result when you believe the truth about who you are and then do what you are supposed to do to renew your mind and walk in the Spirit.

Becoming the Spiritual Person You Want to Be

THE STORY OF ANN SULLIVAN AND HELEN KELLER IS a moving account of the power of God's love at work in and through His people. What does it take to be such a vessel of your heavenly Father's grace?

DATE:————————————————————————————————

BECOMING THE SPIRITUAL PERSON YOU WANT TO BE

(PAGES 87-89)

What does it take to be the kind of Christian who can love a person whom others call hopeless? What moves us beyond our selfishness to deeds of loving service to God and others?

• First, Christian love and service require a firm grasp of your identity in Christ.

> In your own words, describe who you are in Christ. Begin with "As a child of God, I am...." Then read your words aloud, really hear what you're saying, and rejoice!

————————————————————————————

————————————————————————————

————————————————————————————

————————————————————————————

You can't love like Jesus loved until you accept the reality that, because you are in Christ, you are a partaker of His divine nature.

• Second, you must begin to crucify daily the old sin-trained flesh and walk in accordance with who you are: a child of God filled with His Spirit. This process is called walking in the Spirit (see Gal. 5:16-18). And walking in the Spirit cannot be explained in 10 simple how-to steps.

Why is the fact that it is a process reassuring, frightening, or both?

_____

_____

_____

Instead of trying so hard to nail down all the details of the spiritual life, focus on trusting Christ and then let Him move you along in the right direction. Why try to limit to 10 easy steps what life in Christ, the One who died for you, is all about?

DATE:_____

THREE PERSONS AND THE SPIRIT
(PAGES 89-97)

Although Scripture doesn't outline 10 basic steps for living the spiritual life, God's Word does give us some guidelines and important information. We'll begin by considering the distinction Paul makes between natural persons, spiritual persons and fleshly persons.

• **The Natural Person**—This person is spiritually dead, separated from God and therefore living completely independently of Him. Consequently, the natural person sins as a matter of course.

What was your reaction when you read through the diagram on page 90? What surprises did you find in the descriptions of how living apart from God can affect your mind, body, emotions and will?

_____

_____

_____

At what points (flesh, body, emotions, will or mind) did you see something of yourself before you named Jesus as Lord and Savior?

_____

_____

_____

Thank God for the wholeness He has brought to your life.

_____

_____

_____

• **The Spiritual Person**—At the point of conversion, this person's spirit became united with God's Spirit. As a result, this person lives knowing forgiveness for sin, acceptance in God's family and a sense of personal worth.

The description of the spiritual person on page 93 reflects the ideal. Whom have you known who most closely matches this ideal? What has that person taught you about God? about faith?

_____

_____

_____

At what points (body, emotions, spirit, will or mind) does Figure 5-B (page 92) give you an "after" picture and suggest where God has been at work transforming you from the natural "before" person?

_____

_____

_____

Again, thank God for the wholeness He is bringing to your life.

_____

_____

• **The Fleshly Person**—Notice that the spirit of the fleshly person is identical to that of the spiritual person, but there the similarity ends. Instead of being directed by the Spirit, this believer chooses to follow the impulses of the flesh.

Review the description of the fleshly person on page 94. What did you learn about your tendencies to follow the impulses of the flesh rather than the Spirit?

_____

_____

_____

Which of the following words describe your feelings about yourself and about life: inferiority, insecurity, inadequacy, guilt, worry and doubt?

_____

_____

_____

According to the text (see page 96), what does your answer to the preceding question tell you about yourself?

_____

_____

_____

• Believers struggle with the behavior aspect of their growth when they are still struggling with the belief aspect—who they are in Christ.

Consider how you are feeling about yourself and about life (inferior, insecure, inadequate, guilty, worried, or doubtful to some degree). Look up the following Scriptures and choose one of the relevant verses to start memorizing this week.

Inferiority—Ephesians 2:6
Insecurity—Hebrews 13:5
Inadequacy—Philippians 4:13
Guilt—Romans 8:1
Worry—Philippians 4:6
Doubt—James 1:5

Most believers live somewhere between the mountaintop of spiritual maturity (Figure 5-B on page 92) and the depths of fleshly behavior (Figure 5-C on page 94). Walking in the Spirit is key to the process of transformation, which makes God's people more spiritual.

• So why are so few Christians enjoying the abundant, productive life we have inherited through Christ?

> One reason is that victory over sin comes more easily as we mature in our faith. Another reason is that our tendency is to live as though Satan and his dark realm don't exist. What are your thoughts about Satan and his power? Are you ignorant? Are you looking for him behind every bush? Or are you aware of his existence and rely on the armor of God to protect you (see Eph. 6:10f)? Explain and support your answer, and know that chapter 9 focuses on this topic.

_____

_____

_____

Satan takes an active role in opposing our spiritual growth, but it's a role we can stand strong against when we understand the parameters of the Spirit-filled walk.

DATE:_____

PARAMETERS OF THE SPIRIT-FILLED WALK
(PAGES 97-106)

No matter how mature you may feel your faith is, you can never be productive for God's kingdom unless you are walking in the Spirit. Again, there is no magic formula or list of foolproof steps for how to do this, but the Bible does help us see what the Spirit-filled walk is and what it is not.

• Know that there is an element of mystery to walking in the Spirit because it is more a relationship than a regimen.

> What rules for your faith did you begin with or are you beginning with?

_____

_____

> What good purpose did or do these rules serve?

_____

_____

_____

Explain how you have moved beyond (or how you hope to move beyond) these rules to a personal relationship with God.

_____

_____

_____

• **What the Spirit-filled Walk Is Not**—Paul clearly teaches that walking in the Spirit is not license. It is not undisciplined freedom that leads to abusing a privilege. It is not doing anything you want to do. Being led by the Spirit means being free to live a responsible, moral life.

When have you learned that what appears to be an act of freedom can lead to bondage?

_____

_____

_____

How have you found true freedom by walking with Christ? Give an example as Neil did to the questioning high-school student on pages 99-100.

_____

_____

_____

Walking by the Spirit is also not legalism. When have you been the victim of legalism—other imposed or self-imposed? Or when have you been legalistic and judgmental in your attitude toward fellow believers?

_____

_____

_____

What have you learned about the relationship between doing the right Christian things and a person's faith? Do daily Bible study, faithful prayer and regular church attendance guarantee a Spirit–filled walk? Explain why or why not.

_____

_____

Walking with the Spirit is not legalism or license. The Bible's teachings are not to be used as hammers or ignored as irrelevant. Instead, within the confines of God's law, we are free to nurture a spirit-to-Spirit relationship with God, which is the essence of walking in the Spirit.

• **What the Spirit-filled Walk Is**—The Spirit-filled walk is characterized by liberty. As a believer, you are free to choose to walk according to the Spirit or according to the flesh.

> Walking according to the Spirit is not passive but neither is it frenzied. It is walking, not sitting passively and not running endlessly. Which extreme do you tend to lean to and why? Talk to God about your hesitation to take a step forward or your tendency to be busy in an attempt to be more spiritual.

_____

_____

_____

> What was your reaction to the description of being yoked to Jesus (see pages 102-103)? Which of your needs does that description speak to? What message about service did you need to hear? Thank God for the privilege of being yoked to His Son in a relationship of rest and in service to the Kingdom.

_____

_____

The key to a restful relationship yoked with Jesus is to learn from Him and to open yourself to His gentleness and humility. That yoke is also key to serving God. Nothing will ever be accomplished if you and the Lord don't walk together.

• **Walking by Being Led**—When Jesus describes Himself as the Good Shepherd (see John 10:14), He is speaking to our need to be led in our walk of faith.

> Do you struggle with the thought that you are a sheep in need of a shepherd? Why or why not?

_____

_____

Western shepherds drive their flocks while shepherds in the Holy Land—the shepherds Jesus would have referred to—lead their sheep. Why is this difference between being driven and being led significant to you personally?

_____

_____

_____

Thank God that He leads! And He leads hoping that you'll choose to follow. God won't make you walk in the Spirit, and the devil can't make you walk in the flesh, although he'll certainly tempt you to do so.

• **The Proof Is in the Fruit**—How can you know if you're being led by the Spirit or the flesh? Look at your behavior, the fruit of your choices.

According to Galatians 5:22,23, what is the fruit of the Spirit-filled life?

_____

_____

_____

Do the traits you just listed describe your behavior in the last 24 hours? And what does your answer to this question tell you about your relationship with Jesus right now?

_____

_____

_____

• When we discover that we are following the flesh instead of the Spirit, we must admit it and correct it—a simple step, but not always an easy one. When you confess your failures, the scope of your confession should only be as broad as the scope of your offense—and that scope always includes God.

Is it hard for you to admit your failures and confess your sins? Why? Talk to God about that and ask Him to be at work in you.

_____

_____

• The process of restoring a relationship through confession and forgiveness is a step of spiritual growth—and your role as a Christian is to model growth, not perfection.

> Why would admitting your failings be a greater encouragement to people who don't yet know Christ than your efforts to appear perfect?

> _____

> _____

> _____

> Do you hesitate to confess your sins to others? Is it an issue of not trusting that you will be forgiven or accepted? Is it an issue of pride? Is it an issue of being blind to your failures? Again, talk to God and ask Him to transform your heart.

> _____

> _____

> _____

Walking according to the Spirit occurs when you choose to follow the Spirit instead of the temptations of the flesh. When you stray from that path, you can admit your missteps and begin anew in the freedom of God's gracious forgiveness.

DATE: _____

LIVING WHAT YOU LEARN

> Review the ideals reflected in "The Spiritual Person" (page 92). Read again the discussion of walking yoked and in tandem with Jesus based on Matthew 11:28-30 (see pages 102-103). Now consider your life today. In what situation can you live out one of the traits of a spiritual person? What set of circumstances calls you to walk more in tandem with Jesus than you are? Put into action your answers to these two questions.

> _____

> _____

> _____

A Word of Prayer

Heavenly Father, I thank You for sending Your Son as my Savior and Shepherd, for that gift of immeasurable love and grace. As I consider all You've given me and my attempts to live a life that honors You, I am aware of how I fall short. Show me where I'm guilty of license, guilty of cheapening Your grace. And show me where I am guilty of legalism toward others in a judgmental attitude or toward myself in demanding perfection. Thank You for Your forgiveness when I stumble and stray. And teach me, Father God, the liberty I may experience in You so I may enjoy a richer relationship with You and greater sensitivity to Your Spirit. I pray in Jesus' name, amen.

Looking Ahead

As a Christian you are free to choose to walk by the Spirit. Satan does not want you to have that freedom and will try to keep you from enjoying the liberty you have in Christ. The more you walk in step with Jesus, however, the better prepared you will be to recognize and resist Satan's deception.

The Power of Positive Believing

W ILMA RUDOLPH WAS BORN WITH MAJOR HEALTH problems that left her crippled, but after exercising her faith, her courage and her body for years, she became an Olympic medalist and Sullivan Award winner. Can faith do such great things for you?

DATE:_____

THE POWER OF POSITIVE BELIEVING

(PAGES 107-109)

• Reconsider Wilma Rudolph's account of faith.

How did you react to the story of Olympian Wilma Rudolph? What message does her story have for you personally?

_____

_____

_____

Give another example of a person you know of or, better yet, know personally whose faith enabled him or her to rise above incredible odds and achieve things other people wouldn't have.

_____

_____

_____

When has your faith enabled you to stand strong in a difficult situation? Be specific.

_____

_____

_____

What current set of circumstances calls for faith that sometimes seems beyond you? Lift that situation before God in prayer, letting Him know what He already knows—that you're struggling to trust Him.

_____

_____

Faith is indispensable to the Christian life. Believing who God is, what He says and what He does is the key into the kingdom of God. Furthermore, faith is the essence of the Christian's day-to-day activity. You received Christ by faith, and now you are to walk in Him by faith.

DATE: _____

THE DIMENSIONS OF DOWN-TO-EARTH FAITH
(PAGES 109-117)

Too often we think of faith as mystical, mysterious and having little practical application for everyday living. Three simple aspects of faith, however, bring it out of the realm of the abstract and into the practical arena where you live.

• First, faith depends on its object. The fact that you claim to believe is not the issue of faith. It's what you believe in or in whom you believe that determines whether or not your faith will be rewarded.

What are some of the objects and people that believers and nonbelievers alike put their faith in during the course of a regular day? Start your list with the example of red lights and other drivers mentioned in the text.

_____

_____

_____

Which of the faith-objects you listed are solid and trustworthy?

_____

_____

What does it mean to you that "Jesus Christ *is* the same yesterday
and today, *yes* and forever" (Heb. 13:8)?

_____

_____

The ultimate faith-object is Jesus Christ. The fact that He never
changes makes Him eminently trustworthy and eternally faithful. Faith
that is dependent upon God is faith that can enable you to do great
things.

• Second, the depth of your faith is determined by the depth of your
knowledge of the object. When we struggle with our faith in God, it's not
because our faith-object is insufficient. It's because we have unrealistic
expectations of God.

Faith in God only fails when we have a faulty understanding of Him.
When has your faith wavered because, as you saw later, you had had
a faulty understanding of God? Be specific.

_____

_____

If your faith is wavering now with regard to a certain situation,
could it be because of a faulty understanding of God? Search the
Scriptures. Seek counsel from a trusted and mature Christian. Talk
to God about your struggle.

_____

_____

The only way to increase your faith is to increase your knowledge of
God. When has learning something about God enabled you to trust
Him more?

_____

_____

_____

The only limit to your faith is your knowledge and understanding of God, which grows every time you read your Bible, memorize a new Scripture verse, participate in a Bible study or meditate on God's truth.

• Third, faith is an action word. Faith without action isn't faith. If we really believe God and His Word, we will do what He says. What we believe determines what we do. If what we profess to believe doesn't affect our walk or our talk, then we really don't believe.

> Reflect on one of the first times you took a step or made a stand in faith. How did you feel beforehand? What did you learn from the experience? What impact did your active faith have on your relationship with God?

> _____

> _____

> _____

> Explain the difference between positive thinking and positive believing. Share your reaction to the distinction. How does the idea of positive believing call you to greater faith?

> _____

> _____

> _____

> Read through the "Twenty Cans of Success" once again (see pages 115-117). Which "can" are you going to open right now? Do so by looking up the Scripture reference given and memorizing it.

> _____

> _____

> _____

Believing that you can succeed at Christian growth and maturity takes no more effort than believing you cannot succeed. So why not believe that you can walk in faith and in the Spirit? Let the "Twenty Cans of Success" do for you what a Bible study can do—expand your knowledge of Almighty God, the object of your faith, and thereby give your faith the opportunity to grow.

DATE:_____

WHAT HAPPENS WHEN I STUMBLE IN MY WALK OF FAITH?

(PAGES 117-122)

Do you worry that God may be ready to give up on you because you stumble and fall instead of walking confidently in Him? Hear these two wonderful truths:

• **God Loves You Just the Way You Are**—The primary truth you need to know about God in order for your faith to remain strong is that His love and acceptance are unconditional.

> Who in your life was among the first to give you a taste of God's unconditional love? Thank God for that person.
>
> _____
>
> _____
>
> _____

> Do you feel that God loves you when your walk of faith is strong, but probably loves you less (if at all) when you're weak and inconsistent? If so, why do you think you have those feelings? And if not, why do you think you are able to rest in God's unconditional love?
>
> _____
>
> _____
>
> _____

> Who in your life right now needs a taste of God's unconditional love and acceptance? What will you do to show him or her that kind of love?
>
> _____
>
> _____

Know that, as your loving heavenly Father, God can and does understand your weakness and forgive your sin, and He'll never stop doing so.

• **God Loves You No Matter What You Do**—Of course God wants His people to be good, but He has made a provision for our failure through His Son, Jesus Christ, so that His love continues no matter how often we fail (see 1 John 2:1,2). Thanks to the powerful advocate you have in Jesus Christ, God has no reason not to love you and accept you completely, no matter what you do or how you fail.

> What have you done that you feel is reason enough for God to stop loving you?

_____

_____

_____

> Turn your answer to the preceding question into a prayer of confession and then read aloud this truth: "No matter what I do in life, God is always going to love me. He may not approve of everything I do, but He's always going to love me."

_____

_____

_____

Jesus Christ has cancelled the debt of your sins—past, present and future. No matter what you do or how you fail, and despite the lies Satan would have you believe, God has no reason not to love you and accept you completely.

DATE:_____

LIVING WHAT YOU LEARN

> As Paul teaches in Romans 10:17 ("Faith comes from hearing, and hearing by the word of Christ"), the only way to increase your faith is to increase your knowledge of God. What will you do to increase your knowledge of God? Set some goals—long range and short range—regarding church attendance, reading the Bible, attending a Bible study, meditating on God's Word and memorizing passages from Scripture. Find someone who will encourage you, hold you accountable and, even better, join you in your efforts. Then identify the step you will take this week.

_____

_____

_____

A WORD OF PRAYER

God of love and faithfulness, I've been reminded of some
wonderful truths in this chapter, and I offer my thanksgiving
and praise! It's exciting to think that the only limit to my
faith is my knowledge and understanding of You, and it's also
very convicting. Forgive me for my laziness, for not making
time to study the Bible and get to know You better, for not
being willing to spend time reading Your Word—for it is
Your Word, God, that will teach me more about who You
are. Despite all I have yet to learn about You, God, even now
I praise You for being eminently trustworthy and eternally
faithful and for extending to me Your unconditional and eternal love and acceptance. What a privilege and joy to be Your
loved child. May I share the love You give to me with others
so that they, too, may come to know You better. I pray in
Jesus' name, amen.

LOOKING AHEAD

God wants you to accept your identity in Him and live as a child of God
should. But even when you forget who you are, He still loves you. He
wants you to walk in the Spirit, but even when you stumble and stray, He
still loves you. That unconditional, unending love enables you to live out
what you believe, walk in the Spirit, and by your life, invite others to
come along.

CHAPTER SEVEN

You Can't Live Beyond What You Believe

A BASIC TRUTH ABOUT YOUR SPIRITUAL LIFE—and an underlying premise of this book—is that your Christian walk is the direct result of what you believe about God and yourself. And, as the title of this chapter says, you can't live beyond what you believe about God and yourself.

DATE:_____

YOU CAN'T LIVE BEYOND WHAT YOU BELIEVE

(PAGES 123-125)

• The story of Karl's tee shot that opens this chapter in the text (see page 123) illustrates an important aspect of the life of faith: If your faith is off, your walk will be off. If your walk is off, you can be sure it's because your faith is off.

> When have you experienced the first part of this statement—that if your faith is off, your walk will be off? Describe that experience and how you got your faith back on track.

_____

_____

_____

_____

• Walking by faith simply means that you function in daily life on the basis of what you believe.

> Think about a typical day. How does what you believe guide what you do as a spouse, friend, parent, homemaker and/or worker? Be as specific as possible.

> _____

> _____

> _____

> Was the preceding question difficult for you to answer? If so, what does that suggest about your faith and your walk of faith?

> _____

> _____

> _____

> What difference does walking by faith make in your life as a believer? Compare, for instance, how you make decisions, choose a profession, deal with newspaper headlines or cope with personal loss to the way nonbelievers do those things.

> _____

> _____

> _____

• If you haven't done so already, complete the eight questions that comprise the "Personal Worth Appraisal" form (see page 125).

> Look at how you completed the eight sentences. What do your answers show you about yourself?

> _____

> _____

> How well does what you think about these eight values line up with what God says? In other words, what do your answers show you about your walk of faith?

> _____

> _____

> _____

If what you believe about success, significance, fulfillment, satisfaction, happiness, fun, security and peace does not line up with what God teaches about them and their source, your walk of faith will be off to the same degree that your belief is off.

DATE:_____

FEELINGS ARE GOD'S RED FLAG OF WARNING
(PAGES 125-132)

But how can you know if what you believe is right? You can know because God has designed human beings with a feedback system so that we can know on a moment-by-moment basis if our beliefs are properly aligned with His truth. That feedback system is our emotions.

• **Anger Signals a Blocked Goal**—Anger is the first emotional signpost that can alert you that you may be cherishing a faulty goal based on a wrong belief.

> Think about times when you have felt angry and evaluate the preceding statement. Were you angry because one of your goals was blocked? If so, what was that goal?

> _____

> _____

> _____

> Was your goal faulty? If so, what wrong belief (a belief counter to what God teaches) was it based on?

> _____

> _____

> _____

> Any goal that can be blocked by forces you can't control is not a healthy goal because your success in that arena is out of your hands. Do you agree? Why or why not?

> _____

> _____

> _____

Now evaluate your main two or three goals in life. Are they healthy? Why or why not?

_____

_____

_____

Feelings of anger should prompt us to reexamine what we believe and the goals we have formulated to live out those beliefs.

• **Anxiety Signals an Uncertain Goal**—When you feel anxious in a task or relationship, your anxiety may be signalling the uncertainty of a goal you have chosen.

When has your anxiety indeed signalled a goal that you later realized you shouldn't have been pursuing? Be specific about the situation and the lesson you learned.

_____

_____

_____

• **Depression Signals an Impossible Goal**—When there is no physical cause for it, depression can be a signal that your goal, no matter how spiritual or noble, may never be reached.

When, if ever, have you experienced feelings of depression because you were working toward an impossible goal? Be specific about the goal and how you resolved your depression.

_____

_____

_____

Sometimes the depression resulting from working toward an impossible goal is related to a wrong concept of God (see King David's words in Psalm 13:1,2). When, if ever, has your depression been linked to a wrong idea about God?

_____

_____

_____

David moved away from his wrong concept of God and its accompanying depression (see Psalm 13:5,6; 43:5). What does David's example teach you? What hope does it give you?

_____

_____

_____

Again, depression often signals that you are desperately clinging to a goal you have little or no chance of achieving, and that's not a healthy goal.

• **Wrong Responses to Those Who Frustrate Goals**—When your self-worth hinges on the achievement of a goal that can be blocked or that is uncertain or impossible, how do you respond to those who frustrate your goals? Many people try to control or manipulate the people or circumstances that stand in their way.

> When have you attempted to control or manipulate certain circumstances or people who were keeping you from reaching certain goals? Consider the experiences you've already shared in this lesson.
>
> _____
>
> _____
>
> _____
>
> What happened as a result of your attempts to control and/or manipulate? What lessons did you learn from these experiences?
>
> _____
>
> _____
>
> _____

Why do people try to control others? Because they believe (falsely) that their self-worth is dependent on other people and circumstances. But when they are unable to control, they become bitter, angry, resentful, or martyred. The solution for this, and the lesson for you, is to adjust your goals and learn who you are in Christ.

DATE:_____

HOW CAN I TURN BAD GOALS INTO GOOD GOALS?
(PAGES 132-135)

• A faith-stretching question opens this section: If God wants something done, can it be done? In other words, if God has a goal for your life, can it be blocked? Is its fulfillment uncertain or impossible?

> Why does it make sense that the goal your Creator God has for your life cannot be blocked?
>
> _____
>
> _____
>
> _____
>
> No goal God has for your life is impossible or uncertain. Nor can it be blocked. For what area of your life does this fact give you hope?
>
> _____
>
> _____
>
> _____

Just as you wouldn't give your child a task he or she couldn't accomplish, God doesn't assign you goals you can't achieve. His goals for you are possible, certain and achievable. The only requirement for success is your response.

• **Goals vs. Desires**—The secret to achieving God's goals is learning to distinguish a godly goal from a godly desire.

> A godly goal reflects God's purposes for your life and doesn't depend on people or circumstances beyond your ability or right to control. The only person who can block a godly goal or render it uncertain or impossible is you. What godly goal(s) do you have for your life?
>
> _____
>
> _____
>
> _____

A godly desire depends on the cooperation of other people, the success of events and/or the existence of favorable circumstances that you cannot control. (You cannot base your self-worth on these desires, no matter how godly they are, because you cannot control their fulfillment.) What are some of the godly desire(s) that you have for your life?

_____

_____

_____

When desires are elevated to goals and those goals are frustrated, you can experience anger, anxiety and depression. When has that happened to you? (Perhaps you didn't recognize the situation as such at the time, but now looking back through this lens you can see what was happening.) What did you learn from the situation(s)?

_____

_____

_____

It's important to be sure that goals are goals, not elevated desires. One reason is that dealing with the disappointment of unmet desires is a lot easier than dealing with the anger, anxiety and depression of unreached goals, which are based on wrong beliefs.

DATE:_____

GODLY GOALS CENTER ON CHARACTER DEVELOPMENT
(PAGES 135-138)

When you align your goals with God's goals and your desires with God's desires, you will rid your life of a lot of anger, anxiety and depression. Such alignment will be easier when you acknowledge that God's basic goal for your life is character development: becoming the person God wants you to be.

• Becoming the person God wants you to be is clearly a godly goal. As such, no one can block it except you. But along the way you can be sure to encounter distractions, diversions, disappointments, trials, temptations and traumas that will disrupt the process.

Life's distractions, diversions, disappointments, trials, temptations and traumas are a means of achieving your supreme goal of Christian maturity (see Rom. 5:3-5; Jas. 1:2-4). How have the distractions, diversions, disappointments, trials, temptations and traumas of your life helped your faith mature? Give three or four examples.

_____

_____

_____

What current distraction, diversion, disappointment, trial, temptation or trauma can you look at as a means of growing in your faith? What do you think God would have you learn in this situation?

_____

_____

_____

Perhaps the greatest service performed by the trials and tribulations in our lives is to reveal wrong goals. When has this proved true in your own life? When have life's hard times revealed to you the wrongness of your goals? Be specific about the circumstances and the goal(s) you were able to adjust after the experience.

_____

_____

_____

Is there an easier way to become God's person than by enduring trials and persevering through hard times? Believers who have gone before you will tell you that trials and hard times serve as fertile soil for spiritual growth. God may have already taught you that fact firsthand.

DATE: _____

LIVING WHAT YOU LEARN

Review the important distinctions between godly desires and godly goals (see pages 132-138, especially page 133). With that fresh in your mind, evaluate your goals. Are they goals or, more accurately, are they desires? If you've never really set goals for yourself, let this be the opportunity to do so. Godly goals and desires help guide our growth in faith. What two or three goals can you establish and align with God's goals for you? Having written down a few goals—be they long-held ones or newly formulated ones in light of the points in this chapter—determine which one you will begin to work towards and what your first step will be, and then take that step!

_____

_____

_____

A Word of Prayer

Almighty and gracious God, I've read that if my faith is off,

my walk will be off and that if my walk is off, my faith is off.

Show me in these quiet moments where my walk is not what

You would have it be and where my beliefs are not accurate.

I've also read that anger, anxiety and depression can alert me

to faulty goals. Again I ask that You would open my eyes and

show me which goals I'm pursuing are in line with Yours.

May my goals be the goals You would have for me. And,

heavenly Father, may my sense of self-worth be based on the

value You give me as Your child in Christ. Finally, God, may

the overarching goal of my life be to become the person You

want me to be. Teach me, guide me, mold me. I pray in Jesus'

name, amen.

Looking Ahead

God's basic goal for your life is character development: becoming the person He wants you to be. And, in the Bible, He offers some basic guidelines for your walk of faith, the walk that will help you reach that goal.

CHAPTER EIGHT

God's Guidelines for the Walk of Faith

HOW DO YOU BECOME THE PERSON God wants you to be? By walking the walk of faith. The Bible offers important guidelines for doing just that.

DATE:_____

GOD'S GUIDELINES FOR THE WALK OF FAITH

(PAGES 139-141)

• Neil's special breakfast of eggs, sausage and muffins never materialized when his admirable goal was blocked.

> When has one of your goals been blocked? Give two or three examples and let them range in importance from your child deciding to be the lead guitarist in a rock band instead of a doctor, to getting to work late because of traffic.

_____

_____

_____

_____

_____

How did you respond emotionally to your foiled plans and blocked goals? What thoughts went through your mind?

_____

_____

_____

Often our self-worth is tied up with reaching the goals we set for ourselves. When that's the case, life can be a real roller-coaster ride. The only way to get off the roller coaster is to walk by faith according to the truth of God's Word.

DATE: _____

PROPER GUIDELINES LEAD TO A PROPER WALK
(PAGES 141-153)

As we've seen, our walk of faith will be off to the same degree that our beliefs about success, significance, fulfillment, satisfaction, happiness, fun, security and peace are off. So let's see what the Bible teaches about these areas of belief. These lessons from God's Word may help you make some vital adjustments to your walk of faith.

• **Success (Key Concept: Goals)**—Success is directly related to goals. If you're having trouble reaching your goals, it's probably because you're working on the wrong goals.

> A good summary of God's goal for you, His child, is found in 2 Peter 1:3-10, and that goal begins with who you are, based on what God has already done for you. God has given you "life and godliness," and now your job is to diligently adopt God's character goals and apply them to your life. List the seven goals mentioned in 2 Peter 1:5-7. Next to each, give an example from your life where you can work toward that goal (for instance, your income tax return may give you the opportunity to work towards moral excellence).

_____

_____

_____

_____

_____

Remember Joshua? His success hinged entirely on his obedience even when God's plan (to march around Jericho for seven days) sounded quite foolish. What lesson does Joshua offer you and to what current situation in your life can you apply that lesson?

_____

_____

_____

Focusing on God's goals (moral excellence, knowledge, self-control, perseverance, godliness, brotherly kindness and love) will lead to ultimate success, success on God's terms.

• **Significance (Key Concept: Time)**—Time is the true test of significance. What is forgotten in time is of little significance. What is remembered for eternity is of great significance.

When has a brother or sister in the Lord done something for you that he or she said was nothing but was in fact instrumental in your walk of faith? Be specific, and then reflect on the definition of significance given above.

_____

_____

_____

What activities are you involved in that will be remembered for eternity? Answer that question knowing that there is no such thing as a lowly child of God!

_____

_____

_____

What we do and say for Christ, no matter how insignificant it seems in this world, will last forever. And that is "significance."

• **Fulfillment (Key Concept: Role Preference)**—Fulfillment in life comes when you discover your unique God-given abilities and use them to edify others and glorify the Lord.

What does the world promise as the means to fulfillment? Which of these things have you realized, from personal experience, doesn't make good on that promise?

_____

_____

_____

God has a unique place of ministry for each of us, and your greatest fulfillment will come from accepting and occupying, to the best of your ability, God's unique place for you. What can you do today to be God's representative in the following settings?
   Your home
   Your workplace
   Your neighborhood
   Your church
   Your community
   The places you run errands

_____

_____

_____

_____

Find fulfillment in life by deciding to be an ambassador for Christ in the world, in *your* world—and that means at home, in your neighborhood, at work, at school, in your community, wherever you encounter people who don't yet know the Lord and fellow believers whom you can encourage and support.

• **Satisfaction (Key Concept: Quality)**—Satisfaction comes from living righteously and seeking to improve the quality of relationships, projects, products and activities with which you're involved. Satisfaction is a quality issue, not a quantity issue.

When have you experienced the truth that greater satisfaction comes with doing a few things well rather than from doing many things hastily?

_____

_____

_____

Look at your life through the lens of the statement "Satisfaction is a quality issue, not a quantity issue." What does this suggest about how to eliminate some of the dissatisfaction you may currently be feeling?

_____

_____

_____

The key to personal satisfaction is not in broadening your responsibilities but in deepening them through a commitment to quality.

• **Happiness (Key Concept: Wanting What You Have)**—The world says that happiness is having what we want. God says, "Happy is the person who wants what he or she has" (see Matt. 6:31-33).

It's tempting to believe that things we don't have will bring us happiness. This faulty thinking results in discontentment. Change your focus and spend a few minutes now counting your blessings. List some of the many blessings God has given you.

_____

_____

Was Christ on your list of blessings? Explain in your own words why you already have everything you need to make you happy forever when you have Christ, and let that explanation be a prayer of thanksgiving.

_____

_____

If you really want to be happy, learn to be thankful for what you have, not greedy for what you don't have.

• **Fun (Key Concept: Uninhibited Spontaneity)**—Simply put, fun is uninhibited spontaneity, and the secret to enjoying uninhibited spontaneity as a Christian is removing any inhibitors.

What is your idea of fun?

_____

_____

When has (or does) people-pleasing (an inhibitor) interfered with your fun? Be specific about the inhibitor (pride, insecurity, the need to be accepted, a desire to protect your image, etc.).

_____

_____

_____

Know that you'll find a lot more fun in pleasing the Lord than in trying to please people, so ask God to help you let go of any need to please others, protect a reputation, or maintain a certain form of false decorum.

• **Security (Key Concept: Relating to the Eternal)**—The key to experiencing security in your life is to depend on things eternal, not things temporal over which you have no control.

Think about times when you've felt insecure. What temporal thing(s) were you depending on?

_____

_____

_____

Read through Romans 8:35-39 and replace some of the general categories listed (troubles, hardships, persecutions, powers, or circumstances of the present [see vv. 35,38]) with some specifics from your life. Consider then the rhetorical question: How much more secure can you get than God's promise that none of these things you listed can separate you from the love of Christ?

_____

_____

_____

Security only comes from relating to that which is anchored in eternity. The greatest sense of security you can experience comes with taking a firm grip on values and relationships that will endure indefinitely.

• **Peace (Key Concept: Resolving the Internal Conflict)**—The key to experiencing peace is understanding that peace is primarily an internal issue. After all, nobody can guarantee external peace because nobody can control other people or circumstances.

When you named Jesus as your Lord and Savior, you received the gift of peace *with* God. The peace *of* God, however, is something you need to appropriate daily. What does "the peace *of* God" mean to you? Give an example or two of when you have experienced it.

_____

_____

_____

You can control the inner world of your thoughts, emotions and will by allowing the peace of God to rule in your heart on a daily basis. What do you do to access the peace that God gives?

_____

_____

Know that personal worship, prayer and interaction with God's Word provide access to the peace of God, the peace that passes understanding (see Phil. 4:7).

DATE: _____

LIVING WHAT YOU LEARN

As you've read about these eight categories and examined your walk of faith through the lens that they provide, what have you discovered about why you do the things you do? What beliefs do you need to adjust? Which belief will you work on transforming this week?

_____

_____

_____

A WORD OF PRAYER

Heavenly Father, I know that when You call Your people to do something, You also empower them, and that's what this chapter has done. Thank You for the perspective and encouragement it has given me on my walk of faith and on how You would have me walk. Lord, may Your goals for me be my goals. Help me to develop the moral excellence, knowledge of God, self-control, perseverance, godliness, brotherly kindness and Christian love that You want to characterize Your people.

May I find significance in doing things that touch eternity, fulfillment as I represent You in the situations You have placed me in, satisfaction in doing things for You and doing them well, and happiness in my greater awareness of the many blessings You have showered upon me. May I find fun in the gift of life as I stop worrying about my image and other people's thoughts, security in You and You alone and the peace that comes from knowing You.

Help me, Father God, to adjust my beliefs so that my actions will follow and my walk of faith will indeed bring honor and glory to You. I pray in Jesus' name, amen.

LOOKING AHEAD

Are you ready to change your belief system so that your walk of faith will be on God's track? Winning the battle for your mind will be an important step in that direction.

Winning the Battle for Your Mind

Untold numbers of Christians are spiritually unaware and defeated in their lives. They don't realize that there is a battle going on for their mind. They are children of God, but they are defeated children, unwitting victims of the deceiver.

DATE:————————————————————————————

WINNING THE BATTLE FOR YOUR MIND

(PAGES 155-156)

• A Christian's walk of faith can be—and often is—stymied by the arch-enemy of faith: a mind plagued by demonic suggestion.

> What was your reaction—emotional and intellectual—to Shelley's story? How credible do you find her experience?

————————————————————————————

————————————————————————————

————————————————————————————

————————————————————————————

————————————————————————————

————————————————————————————

You may or may not struggle to accept the very real power of Satan and his demons. If you don't accept the power of the demonic realm, why do you hesitate to believe what is taught in Scripture? If you acknowledge Satan and his efforts to trip up believers, how did you come to understand that truth?

_____

_____

_____

What do you do to battle Satan when you recognize his efforts to deceive and debilitate?

_____

_____

_____

When struggling believers come to understand their identity in Christ, and realize that they can be transformed by the renewing of their mind, they can experience freedom just as Shelley did.

DATE:_____

GOD'S WAY VS. MAN'S WAY
(PAGES 157-160)

Faith is God's way to live, and reason is man's way. But faith and man's ability to reason are often in conflict. God is a rational God and He does work through our rational ability. The problem is that our ability to reason is limited (see Isa. 55:9).

• We can live God's way and operate by faith (Plan A), or we can live our way and operate by our limited ability to reason (Plan B).

The strength of Plan A in your life is determined by your personal conviction that God's way is always right and by how committed you are to obeying Him. When has your conviction that God's way is always right wavered? What specific issues have moved you to question God's way?

_____

_____

The strength of Plan B is determined by the amount of time and energy you invest in entertaining thoughts that are contrary to God's Word. Are you, for instance, currently establishing an escape route in case God's plan fails? In other words, are you contemplating your own plans on how to live your life instead of investing time and energy in seeking God's plan and asking Him to help you live it out?

_____

_____

_____

When you vacillate between God's Plan A and your Plan B, your spiritual growth will be stunted and your daily experience as a Christian will be marked by disillusionment, discouragement and defeat.

• The moment a Christian wife begins to think that she should get a part-time job in case her marriage doesn't work out, she cannot help but take something away from her wholehearted commitment to Plan A. The more she thinks about Plan B, the better the chances that she's going to need it. Where do such Plan B thoughts come from?

First, your flesh still generates humanistic thoughts and ideas. God gave you a new nature when you accepted His Son as Lord and Savior, but the old Plan B habits and thought patterns are still part of your flesh. On what issues does your flesh speak out most vocally and call you to live independently of God?

_____

_____

_____

Plan B thoughts come from the flesh and, second, from the devil. Satan and his demons are actively trying to distract you from your walk of faith by establishing negative, worldly patterns of thought in your mind. What negative thought patterns, past or present, might have been the result of Satan's efforts?

_____

_____

_____

The essence of the battle for your mind is the conflict between Plan A, living by faith in God, and Plan B, living by the flesh as it is influenced by past patterns, the world and the devil. Although you may feel quite helpless, you need to realize that you are the one who determines the winner in every skirmish between Plan A and Plan B.

D<small>ATE</small>:_____

S<small>TRONGHOLDS</small> A<small>RE THE</small> P<small>RIME</small> T<small>ARGET OF</small> O<small>UR</small> W<small>ARFARE</small>
(<small>PAGES</small> 160-166)

• The battle for your mind is not fought on the plane of human ingenuity or ability. You can't outsmart or outmuscle the flesh or the devil on your own. You need weapons of the Lord to overcome the strongholds established in your mind—established either through repetition over time or through one-time traumatic experiences.

> At this point in the chapter, what strongholds in the mind can you identify for yourself?
>
> _____
>
> _____
>
> _____
>
> Consider now the sources of the strongholds of the mind.

• **Environmental Stimulation**—Every day before you came to Christ you were influenced by and preconditioned to conform to the hostile world in which we all live.

> What did *brief stimulation*—individual events, situations, places and personal encounters you experienced, books you read, movies you saw, music you listened to and traumatic events you witnessed—teach you about how to cope, resolve conflicts and live in the world?
>
> _____
>
> _____
>
> _____
>
> _____
>
> What did *prevailing stimulation*—the influence of your family, your friends and peers, your neighborhood, your teachers and your job—

teach you about how to survive, cope and succeed in this world
apart from God?

_____

_____

_____

Evaluate the validity and the morality of the environmental stimulation you have experienced and its impact on you.

_____

_____

_____

When you became a Christian your sins were washed away, but your
predisposition to think and behave certain ways (which you developed as
you adjusted to your environment) remained ingrained in your flesh. That
is why we need to be transformed by the renewing of our minds (see
Rom. 12:2).

• **Temptation**—Whenever you are stimulated to conform to Plan B
instead of God's Plan A, you are experiencing temptation.

> The essence of all temptation is the invitation to live independently
> of God and fulfill legitimate needs in the world, the flesh or the
> devil instead of in Christ. What invitations are you especially sus-
> ceptible to?

_____

_____

_____

Satan knows how to tempt you away from dependency on Christ. He
knows where you are vulnerable, and that's where he attacks. Your temptations will be unique to your area of vulnerability.

• **Consideration and Choice**—The moment you are tempted to meet
your needs in the world rather than in Christ, you must make a decision.

> God provides a way for you to escape every temptation, but that
> opportunity for escape must be seized the moment you are tempted.
> When have you, like Cathy of the "Cathy" comic strip, let your
> unchecked thoughts carry you away like a runaway freight train,

leading you to do exactly what you didn't want to do initially? Give a specific example.

_____

_____

_____

When have you been tempted but taken that thought captive and acted in obedience to Christ? Explain what occured. (Did God give you strength at the point you needed it? Did you receive freedom once you decided on God's Plan A course of action? Did you walk away from the temptation?)

_____

_____

If we don't capture the tempting thought when it first arises, it will probably capture us!

• **Action, Habit and Stronghold**—When you pause to consider a temptation and then make the Plan B choice, you will find yourself acting on that choice and owning that behavior. And you are responsible for that action because you failed to take the tempting thought captive. If you continue to do that action for six weeks, it becomes a habit or, in this context, a stronghold.

Hostility, inferiority, manipulation, homosexuality, anorexia and bulimia are strongholds. Any knee-jerk response that directs your thinking and acting in a negative, Plan B way is a stronghold in your mind. Now, having learned more about strongholds, identify any strongholds that exists in your mind.

_____

_____

_____

Perhaps it still isn't easy to identify strongholds in your mind. Considering possible sources of strongholds may help.

_____

_____

_____

A woman who was raped while a siren wailed in the background went into a deep depression every time she heard a siren. Has such a brief and traumatic encounter resulted in a stronghold in your mind? If so, identify that stronghold.

_____

_____

_____

Three brothers learned their various responses to hostile behavior (fighting, appeasing and running away) growing up with an alcoholic father. What strongholds in your mind are the result of the prevailing atmosphere of your life?

_____

_____

_____

Imagine life without these strongholds you've identified. How would life be different for you?

_____

_____

_____

Any negative thoughts and actions you cannot control spring from a stronghold. Somewhere in the past you consciously or unconsciously formed a pattern of thinking and behaving that now controls you. Simply putting on the armor of God at this point won't solve your dilemma.

DATE: _____

IN ORDER TO WIN THE BATTLE FOR YOUR MIND,
YOU NEED A STRATEGY
(PAGES 166-169)

If the strongholds in your mind are the result of conditioning, know that you can be reconditioned by the renewing of your mind. Through the preaching of God's Word, Bible study and personal discipleship you can stop being conformed to this world and experience the transformation of the renewing of your mind.

• You face more than just negative conditioning. You're also up against the devil who is scheming to fill your mind with thoughts that are opposed to God's plan for you.

In 2 Corinthians 10:5, Paul writes "We are taking every thought captive to the obedience to Christ." Thoughts need to be taken captive because they are the enemy's thoughts. Comment on that fact. What kind of encouragement do you find in this truth? How does it help you as you consider trying to take thoughts captive?

_____

_____

_____

Satan's strategy is to introduce his thoughts into your mind and to deceive you into believing that they are yours. Comment on the effectiveness of this strategy and identify two or three times when you have realized later that ideas you thought were your own were actually Satan's.

_____

_____

_____

What do these two truths (i.e., taking thoughts captive and Satan's strategy) help you understand about times in the past when you've chosen Plan B?

_____

_____

_____

In light of these truths, what will you do to be better prepared the next time temptation arises?

_____

_____

If you knew Satan had a certain idea planted in your mind, you'd reject that thought, wouldn't you? Disguising his suggestion as your idea is Satan's primary deception. If Satan can get you to believe a lie, he can control your life. If you fail to take a thought captive in obedience to Christ and instead believe it and act on it, Satan will control you.

DATE: _____

EXPOSE THE LIE AND YOU WIN THE BATTLE

(PAGES 169-173)

Satan's power is in the lie (see John 8:44). Satan has no power over you except what you give him by failing to take every thought captive and thus being deceived into believing his lies.

What kind of deception are you possibly experiencing due to the enemy? His attacks range from voices in one's mind to negative thoughts that interfere with devotions.

Since Satan's primary weapon is the lie, your defense against him is the truth. When you expose Satan's lie with God's truth, his power is broken.

• What is your part in the battle for your mind?

First, you must be transformed by the renewing of your mind (see Rom. 12:2), and that happens when you fill it with God's Word. What are you doing regularly to let "the word of Christ richly dwell within you" (Col. 3:16)?

_____

_____

_____

Second, you must prepare your mind for action (see 1 Pet. 1:13). What imaginings would you do well to dispose of?

_____

_____

_____

In what current situation would you do well to imagine yourself obeying the truth?

_____

_____

_____

_____

Third, take every thought captive in obedience to Christ (see 2 Cor. 10:5). What can you do to keep alert and be sure to capture an idea from Satan—a Plan B thought—when it first arises?

_____

_____

_____

Fourth, turn to God in prayer. Why is this hard to do when Plan B thoughts are challenging your commitment to Plan A?

_____

_____

_____

When you bring Plan B ideas before the Lord in prayer, you are acknowledging God and exposing your thoughts to His truth. That means victory over your enemy, the deceiver.

DATE: _____

LIVING WHAT YOU LEARN

What have you learned about yourself in this chapter? What plan of action do these lessons about yourself call for? You may need to talk to a pastor or counselor about the strongholds you seem to be battling. You may also want to get some suggestions about the kind of further Bible study you can be doing as you work to fill your mind with God's truth. Let this lesson you've just completed empower you as you discover in God's truth the effective weapon you need against Satan and his demons.

_____

_____

_____

_____

A Word of Prayer

Heavenly Father, Your words of truth are like a refreshing wind blowing away the chaff and clearing my mind. Thank You for this perspective on your Plan A versus my too-often-considered Plan B on strongholds in my mind. Thank You that, with Your truth, I can be victorious over Satan's deceptions. God, my thoughts need to be taken captive because Satan often disguises his suggestions as my ideas. Please show me which negative thoughts and behavior patterns are strongholds that Satan uses against me in my walk of faith. Teach me to be vigilant in the analysis of my ideas and diligent in filling my mind with Your truth and turning to You in prayer. God, I want to stand strong in Your truth so that I may experience freedom in You. I pray in Jesus' name, amen.

Looking Ahead

Again, when you expose Satan's lies with God's truth, Satan's power is broken and the victory is yours. Such victory in the battle for your mind is the undisputed inheritance of everyone who is in Christ.

CHAPTER TEN

You Must Be
Real in Order
to Be Right

V ICTORY IN THE BATTLE FOR YOUR MIND is the undisputed inheritance of everyone who is in Christ, and recognizing that there *is* a battle is the first step.

DATE:_____

YOU MUST BE REAL IN ORDER TO BE RIGHT

(PAGES 175-178)

• Review the story of Daisy and then consider these questions.

How does Daisy's story illustrate the chapter title "You Must Be Real in Order to Be Right"? In light of Daisy's experience, explain what that title means.

_____

_____

_____

Why are anger and anxiety perfect footholds for Satan?

_____

_____

_____

_____

Where have you not been—or where are you not being—"real" about your emotions?

_____

_____

_____

Daisy's unresolved anger toward her father and her efforts to cover up her anxieties kept her from spiritual victory, spiritual growth and freedom in Christ. What's keeping you from experiencing these things?

_____

_____

DATE: _____

YOUR EMOTIONS REVEAL YOUR PERCEPTIONS
(PAGES 178-181)

Your emotions play a major role in the process of renewing your mind. If you fail to acknowledge your emotions, you may make yourself a slow-moving target for Satan.

• As we see in Lamentations 3, the prophet Jeremiah's despair changes when his perception of God changes. When Jeremiah recalls God's unceasing lovingkindness and great faithfulness, his emotions follow suit.

When have your emotions clearly been the result of wrong thinking about a situation, a person or God?

_____

_____

_____

How did your thinking get straightened out? What change in emotions did you experience as a result?

_____

_____

_____

You Must Be
Real in Order
to Be Right

• You are not shaped as much by your environment as you are by your perception of your environment. Likewise, life's events don't determine who you are. God determines who you are, but your interpretation of life's events determines how well you handle the pressures of life.

> What did you learn from the story about the real estate loan (see pages 180-181 of the text)? What did this illustration show you about the connection between events, thoughts and emotions?

_____

_____

_____

• If what you believe does not reflect truth, then what you feel does not reflect reality. Even so, you can't simply change or turn off your emotions. The problem that must be addressed is the wrong perception of the situation that is making you feel the way you do. The solution is to adjust your perception of the situation and base it on truth.

> Describe your general state of emotions right now. If you're feeling more negative than positive, consider whether you are thinking wrongly about a certain event. Ask God to give you insight as you adjust your thinking and know that the emotions will follow.

_____

_____

_____

• The order of Scripture is to know the truth, believe it, walk according to it and let your emotions be a product of your obedience.

> Why is it so easy to believe what you feel?

_____

_____

> What will you do to know the truth better so that you can trust truth rather than emotions?

_____

_____

_____

Knowing truth and acting on it comes first. Your emotions follow, but they are more than just a tailgate. They play a vital role in daily life.

DATE:_____

DON'T IGNORE THE WARNING SIGNS OF YOUR EMOTIONS
(PAGES 181-188)

Your emotions are to your soul what your physical feelings are to your body. If you didn't feel the gamut of emotions from anger to joy, from sorrow to delight, your soul would be in trouble. Emotions let you know what is going on inside you.

• Think about your general attitude and reaction toward emotions.

Are you comfortable with people's expressions of emotions? Why or why not?

_____

_____

_____

Are you comfortable expressing emotions? Why or why not?

_____

_____

_____

Why is it significant that God designed emotions?

_____

_____

_____

Just as you have learned to respond to the warnings of physical pain and to the red warning lights on you car's dashboard, you need to learn to respond to your emotions. We'll look at three options.

• **The Duct Tape of Suppression**—Suppression is a conscious denial of feelings. It is the choice not to deal with them, and it is an unhealthy response to your emotions.

Were you taught to suppress your emotions? Describe how you learned that lesson (through modeling, being reprimanded, environmental influences, etc.).

_____

_____

_____

What have been the unhealthy consequences of suppressing your emotions? How have you suffered because other people suppressed their emotions?

_____

_____

_____

Why are you sometimes or even often tempted to suppress certain emotions? Ask God to help free you from this fear and to teach you a better way to deal with your emotions.

_____

_____

Don't cover over your emotions. Suppression isn't good for you, for others or for your relationship with God.

• **The Hammer of Indiscriminate Expression**—Another unhealthy way to respond to emotions is to tell anybody and everybody how you feel.

Do you sometimes choose this option? Describe some of the consequences (personal and interpersonal) of indiscriminately expressing your emotions.

_____

_____

Anger is a prime candidate for indiscriminate expression. How do you deal with anger? Talk to God about how you would like to deal with anger and any other emotions you tend to share indiscriminately. Open your heart to His way.

_____

_____

If you wish to be angry and not sin, then be angry the way Christ was: be angry *at* sin. Turn over the tables, not the money changers.

• **The Tape Measure of Acknowledgment**—If you come to your prayer time feeling angry, depressed or frustrated and then mouth a bunch of pious platitudes as if God doesn't know how you feel, do you think He is pleased? Not unless He's changed His opinion about hypocrisy since the times of the Pharisees!

> Acknowledging your feelings is healthy. Not acknowledging them is unhealthy and hypocritical. What keeps you from acknowledging your feelings?

> Acknowledging your emotions involves being honest and open in front of a few trusted friends. In fact, it is difficult to maintain mental health unless you have at least one person with whom you can be emotionally honest. With whom can you be emotionally honest? Thank God for that person. If there is no one in your life right now with whom you can be emotionally honest, ask God to give you that important friend, and, in the meantime, work on being emotionally honest with God.

So now you understand the importance of emotional honesty and you want to be emotionally honest, but it's unfamiliar territory for you. How do you start? The following guidelines will help.

DATE: _____

EMOTIONAL HONESTY: HOW TO DISH IT OUT AND HOW TO TAKE IT
(PAGES 188-192)

One of the challenges in the area of emotions is learning how to respond to others when they honestly acknowledge their feelings.

• Neil was with the two parents when their son died. Tired and emotionally depleted, Neil had no words of comfort. Instead, he sat there and cried with them. Later, they told him that his tears had let them know of his love.

Why do you think we (or, more specifically, you) always feel the need to respond to someone's emotions with words?

_____

_____

_____

When has someone shown you that he or she understands what you're feeling by crying with you? How did you react to that person's tears?

_____

_____

_____

You don't respond to someone's emotions with words. You respond to emotions with emotions. Your Savior wept, for instance, when grief-stricken Mary and Martha told Him of Lazarus's death.

• It's important to respond to emotions with emotions. It's also important to not take too seriously the words of someone who is expressing his or her emotions honestly.

Why is this a good rule to follow?

_____

_____

_____

How do you want people to respond to you when you're dealing with some intense emotions and needing to talk them out? (Your answer may be a good guideline for you to follow the next time you're with a person who is hurting.)

_____

_____

_____

You weep with those who weep. You don't offer a lecture in response to the rhetorical questions asked out of the depth of their pain.

• Another important point about dealing with emotions is this: Don't forsake love in your eagerness to be honest.

Remember the husband, the wife, the 6:00 dinner and the 7:00 meeting? How would you like to respond if you were the husband? If you were the wife?

_____

_____

_____

What do you do to try to control your tongue so that, when emotions are high, you don't sacrifice love in the name of honesty?

_____

_____

When it comes to acknowledging emotions with your inner circle, honesty is the best policy. But be sure to speak the truth in love (Eph. 4:15).

• When you're dealing with emotions, know your limitations. Be aware that times of high emotions are not times for good decision making. Also, be ready to continue a discussion at a later time before you say something you'll regret.

What emotions tend to push you to make decisions that aren't always the best? Are those emotions signals to you to put off decisions until your emotions have subsided?

_____

_____

_____

Is "May we continue this discussion later?" part of your vocabulary when you're reaching your emotional limits? If so, how has it served you? If not, what can you do to add it to your repertoire?

_____

_____

_____

As human beings, we have limitations, and emotions can push us to those limits. We need to give ourselves permission to acknowledge our limits and stay within the bounds of love and patience when emotions are running high.

• Finally, realize that various physical factors affect your emotional limits.

What physical factors tend to affect your emotional limits?

_____

_____

_____

Which of those factors are you dealing with right now? What are you doing to cope with them?

_____

_____

_____

The important process of renewing your mind includes managing your emotions by managing your thoughts and perceptions. The process also involves acknowledging your feelings honestly and lovingly in your relationships with others.

DATE: _____

LIVING WHAT YOU LEARN

Review the guidelines for emotional honesty and choose which guideline you need to work on the most. Then read through the guidelines for emotional honesty with a person who is affected by your ability to be emotionally honest (a spouse, child, parent, close friend, co-worker, roommate, etc.). Let that person know what you will be working on and ask him or her to work with you and hold you accountable. That person may also want to choose a guideline on which to work.

_____

_____

_____

A Word of Prayer

Creator God, You gave me my emotions so that I can know what is going on inside. Thank You for that gift. Too often, though, I listen to and believe my emotions rather than the truth. At moments when that happens, please bring me back to Your truth so that I can believe it, walk according to it and let my emotions follow. And, Father God, please free me from emotions I have suppressed and/or my tendency to suppress my emotions. Forgive me for times I have indiscriminately expressed my emotions and show me whom I've hurt and need to ask forgiveness of. Give me the courage and sensitivity I need in order to acknowledge my emotions and to support those I care about when they are sharing their emotions. May I reflect Your love as I learn to follow the guidelines for emotional honesty that I've been reading about. And Father, enable me to be emotionally honest with You, as You already know what I'm feeling anyway. I pray in Jesus' name, amen.

Looking Ahead

Responding to your emotions properly is an important step in keeping the devil from gaining a foothold in your life. Sometimes you also need to respond to emotions and emotional wounds left over from the past.

Healing Emotional Wounds from Your Past

ALL OF US HAVE AN EMOTIONAL HISTORY. We've all been hurt along the way, and the emotions from these life experiences can interfere with our spiritual growth.

DATE:_____

HEALING EMOTIONAL WOUNDS FROM YOUR PAST

(PAGES 193-194)

• Reread the story of Cindy and Dan.

What misunderstanding of God's truth was keeping Cindy from leaving behind her identity as a rape victim? See Romans 8:28.

_____

_____

Neil explained to Cindy that God works everything for good, but He doesn't make a bad thing good. How might this truth affect Cindy's emotions?

_____

_____

_____

Where can you apply Neil's explanation of Romans 8:28 to your life? And how can this truth affect your emotions?

_____

_____

_____

Cindy needed to be reminded that she is a child of God and encouraged to see herself as His much-loved daughter instead of as a rape victim. You, too, are a child of God. Remember that as you consider hurts from your past.

DATE: _____

BAD THINGS DO HAPPEN TO GOOD PEOPLE
(PAGES 194-196)

Any number of traumatic, emotional events, varying in intensity, have cluttered your soul with emotional baggage. That baggage can limit your spiritual growth and make you a likely target for the deceptions of Satan. Consider how emotions from the past may be affecting you today.

• As the next two questions will illustrate, years of life experience have etched emotional grooves inside you that produce a decided reaction when a certain topic is introduced.

How did you react to the story of Cindy's rape? What events from your past determined your reaction?

_____

_____

_____

What names evoke a positive emotional reaction from you? What names bring forth negative emotions? Give a few examples of each and say, if you can, why you react as you do.

_____

_____

_____

_____

The long-term emotions that determine your reactions to events and names are primary emotions. The intensity of your primary emotions is determined by your previous life history.

• Review the path from "Previous Life History" to "Secondary Emotion" (see pages 195-196) and then answer these questions.

> When have you experienced the process outlined here? When has a present event triggered a primary emotion? Be specific.

> _____

> _____

> _____

> What did you do to deal with the primary emotion? In other words, what did you do at the "Mental Evaluation" management stage?

> _____

> _____

> _____

> What secondary emotion did you then deal with?

> _____

> _____

> _____

If you handled well the primary and secondary emotions you felt in the experience you just outlined, you may have learned how to resolve conflicts from your past. It's important to learn how to do that so you can deal with the primary and secondary emotions they prompt. Also, resolving previous conflicts keeps emotional baggage from accumulating, weighing you down and even controlling your life.

DATE:_____

LEARNING TO RESOLVE PRIMARY EMOTIONS
(PAGES 196-199)

Some Christians assert that the past isn't important, but those who have experienced major traumas and learned to resolve them in Christ know how devastating the past can be to present reality.

• Our God is a God of light. As such, He brings into the light our wounds from the past so that we can deal with them and be healed.

Which of the ideas in this chapter are new to you? What are your thoughts about the possibility of memories being buried deep within one's subconscious, the past holding a person in bondage, or primary emotions being rooted in events of long ago?

_____

_____

_____

Perhaps these ideas are not unfamiliar to you. You may have even seen God, the Wonderful Counselor, work in your life or in the life of someone close to you. If so, comment on God's timing. How did His revelation of the past correspond with your (or the person's) level of maturity?

_____

_____

_____

Consider praying with David the words of Psalm 139: "Search me, O God, and know my heart; try me and know my anxious thoughts; and see if there be any hurtful way in me, and lead me in the everlasting way" (vv. 23,24). God knows about the hidden hurts within you that you may not be able to see. You can trust Him to be by your side as you feel the emotions from the past and to free you from their effect on your life.

_____

_____

_____

When you ask God to search your heart, He will expose those dark areas of your past and bring them to light—into His healing light—at the right time.

DATE: _____

SEE YOUR PAST IN THE LIGHT OF WHO YOU ARE

(PAGES 199-200)

How does God intend for you to resolve those hurtful experiences from the past?

• You have the privilege of evaluating your past experience in light of who you are now.

> If the hurts happened before you were a believer, you can find hope in the fact that, as a Christian, you are a new creature in Christ. Old things, including the traumas of your past, are passed away. Spend some time now praying about this powerful truth. Ask that God would help you believe in that newness as you deal with emotions and hurts from the past.

_____

_____

_____

> If you were a believer when the trauma(s) occurred, what hope do you find in the promise of Romans 8:28 and the perspective that offered Cindy hope at the beginning of this chapter?

_____

_____

_____

• Remember the relationship between emotions and beliefs? Keep in mind that the intensity of the primary emotion was established by how you perceived the event at the time it happened.

> Explain how this truth can help you deal with the primary emotions rooted in your past.

_____

_____

_____

_____

_____

• When a present event activates a person's primary emotions, that person believes what he or she feels instead of believing what is true. But, again, you have the opportunity to look at past events from the perspective of who you are today.

> People who have been verbally abused by their parents struggle to believe that they are loved unconditionally by Father God. Their primary emotions argue that they are unlovable to a parent figure. They find it hard to believe that they are of great value in Christ. What did you learn from this example of primary emotions, rooted in the past, that contradict today's reality?

> _____

> _____

> _____

> If these people (and maybe you're one of them) began to believe their value in Christ, how would life be different?

> _____

> _____

Perceiving painful events of the past from the perspective of your new identity in Christ (or of your renewed appreciation of that identity) is what starts the process of healing damaged emotions.

DATE: _____

FORGIVE THOSE WHO HAVE HURT YOU IN THE PAST
(PAGES 200-207)

The first step in resolving past conflicts is to evaluate the past in light of who you are in Christ now. The second step is to forgive those who have offended you. And why should you forgive those who have hurt you in the past?

• First, forgiveness is required by God.

> Read again Matthew 6:14,15. Comment on the inclusiveness of the command and what it reflects about the One who issued the command.

> _____

> _____

Like all of God's commands, the command to forgive is given for
your benefit. What happens to us when we don't forgive those who
have hurt us?

_____

_____

_____

• Second, forgiveness is necessary to avoid entrapment by Satan.

Why is lack of forgiveness a foothold for Satan? What can the
deceiver do with that foothold to block your relationship with God?

_____

_____

_____

When have you seen a person entrapped by his or her unwillingness
to forgive? Describe the effects on that person.

_____

_____

_____

• Third, forgiveness is to be the standard operating procedure among all
believers (see Eph. 4:31,32).

Why is forgiveness important in the community of believers?

_____

_____

_____

Why is forgiveness important to the witness of the community of
believers?

_____

_____

_____

There are several reasons why we should forgive those who have hurt
us in the past, but...

• **What Is Forgiveness?**—Let's begin to answer that question by saying what forgiveness is *not*.

Forgiveness is *not* forgetting. Respond to this truth. Is this a new perspective for you? What does it mean about forgiveness you've extended to people in the past?

_____

_____

_____

Forgiveness does *not* mean tolerating sin. When has extending forgiveness meant explaining that you won't tolerate the same offense in the future? Describe how you dealt with or would like to deal with that situation.

_____

_____

_____

Forgiveness does *not* demand revenge or repayment for offenses suffered. You can let the ones who hurt you off your hook because you realize that God does not let them off His hook. Why is it hard to leave justice up to God?

_____

_____

_____

• Forgiveness is not forgetting; it's not tolerating sin; it's not demanding revenge. What then is forgiveness? Forgiveness is resolving to live with the consequences of another person's sin. You can choose to live in bitterness and unforgiveness or in peace and forgiveness. The latter, of course, is God's way.

Describe a time when you found peace once you forgave someone who wronged you.

_____

_____

_____

Now consider an opportunity you now have to forgive someone. What's holding you back? Make this situation a topic of prayer.

_____

_____

_____

Expect positive results when you extend forgiveness to those who have hurt you. In time, you will be able to think about the people who offended you without feeling hurt, angry or resentful.

• **Twelve Steps to Forgiveness**—Nobody really forgives another person without acknowledging the hurt and the hatred that are involved. But until you forgive, that person will continue to hurt you because you have not released yourself from the past. Know that forgiveness is the only way to stop the pain. The text outlines a process for forgiving someone (see pages 203-205).

Which steps in the process surprise you?

_____

_____

_____

Which steps in the process are especially hard for you?

_____

_____

_____

Comment on the wisdom of the steps and why this process proves effective and freeing.

_____

_____

As difficult as these steps can be, know that forgiveness really is the only way to freedom from past hurts.

• **A Second Touch**—In Mark 8:22-26, Jesus heals a blind man. At Jesus' first touch, the man says, "I see men...like trees" (v. 24). When Jesus touches the man a second time, he begins to see people as people.

Why does seeing people as people enable us to forgive them when they hurt us?

_____

_____

Have you ever recognized that a person who hurt you is also some-one who has suffered and been hurt? Did this help you forgive that person?

_____

_____

_____

Where do you need a second touch from the Lord right now? Think about people who have hurt you. Which of those do you need to see more clearly as people?

_____

_____

_____

In a few quiet moments now, ask for a second touch from the Lord that you might see those who hurt you as people who themselves have been hurt. As you do so, know that this second touch is one way God will help you become more the person He wants you to be.

DATE: _____

LIVING WHAT YOU LEARN

You've read through the steps of forgiveness. Now it's time to work through them. After you pray the prayer that follows, get out a blank sheet of paper and list the names of people who have offend-ed and hurt you, and describe the specific wrongs you suffered. With that, you will have taken the first step in the journey toward freedom from past hurts. Then move on to the second step, and don't be afraid to invite a trusted friend or a professional counselor to help you and pray for you at this step or any of the others. What is to be gained by forgiveness is freedom.

A WORD OF PRAYER

All-knowing and all-loving God, I come before you with
David's words on my lips, "Search me, O God" (Ps. 139:23a).
Maybe there is something in my past that, brought to light,
into Your healing light, can mean freedom for me. Show me,
merciful and gentle God, who I need to forgive and of what I
need to forgive them.

Bad things do happen to good people—to Your people, God.
Help me to trust Your love and Your power of redemption as
I look to You to work good from the pain I've experienced.

And, God, as I confront that pain, I hear Your call to forgive
those who have hurt me. I know that Your command to forgive is for my own good, but it's so hard. Yet as Jesus hung
from the cross, He asked You to forgive those who crucified
Him. May I follow His example. Be with me as I work
through the steps of forgiveness. May I be aware of Your
love and protection as I deal with harsh truth and deep pain.
I pray in the precious name of Your Son and my Savior, the
One who forgives and enables me to forgive, amen.

LOOKING AHEAD

Healing emotional wounds from the past will enable you to find victory
over the darkness and freedom in God's light. Dealing with any rejection
you've experienced is also essential to realizing victory.

Dealing with Rejection in Your Relationships

E VERYONE KNOWS WHAT IT feels like to be criticized and rejected at times, and often we know criticism and rejection from the very people we so desperately want to please. All of us have experienced the pain of rejection to some degree.

DATE:_____

DEALING WITH REJECTION IN YOUR RELATIONSHIPS
(PAGES 209-211)

• Most of us haven't suffered the pervasive rejection that Ruby experienced, but each of us has been ignored, overlooked or rejected at times by parents, teachers and friends.

> In the previous chapter you took the first step in the process of forgiveness and listed people who had hurt you. Which of those people inflicted pain, knowingly or unknowingly, by rejecting you?

_____

_____

_____

_____

How has Satan and his demons been using your experiences of being rejected to keep you from believing you are a loved child of God? What lies has Satan taught you and ingrained into your mind?

_____

_____

_____

Since we all know rejection, we all need to be aware that Satan uses those experiences to keep us down. But God, who Himself rejected us until we were accepted by Him in Christ at salvation, is able to free us from the pain of rejection and the false messages that Satan has etched into our minds.

DATE: _____

WHEN YOU ARE CRITICIZED OR REJECTED
(PAGES 211-217)

• Rejection, and the accompanying thoughts and feelings, can be a major deterrent to growth and maturity.

What thoughts and feelings about yourself do you deal with as a result of the times you've been rejected?

_____

_____

_____

How do you think these thoughts and feelings have blocked your growth—spiritually and otherwise?

_____

_____

_____

There are various ways to respond to rejection, and most of us choose one of the three negative options rather than the positive approach.

• **Beat the System**—Some people respond to rejection by learning to compete and scheming to get ahead. Striving to earn acceptance and significance through their performance, these people are characterized by perfectionism, emotional insulation, anxiety and stress. Committed to controlling people and circumstances for their own ends, these beat-the-system people also have a hard time coming under God's authority.

Why is "beat the system" an appealing option for someone who has been rejected?

_____

_____

_____

Do you know someone who fits the above description? Describe the rejection that person experienced and the consequences of this response.

_____

_____

_____

Beat-the-system people are some of the most insecure people you will meet. Sadly, their strategy only delays further and inevitable rejection.

• **Give in to the System**—Most people today respond to rejection by simply giving in to the system. They continue to try to satisfy others, but their failures prompt them to believe that they really are unlovable and that being rejected is understandable. These people tend to blame God for their situation and find it difficult to trust Him.

Why do many people choose this option in response to the rejection they've experienced?

_____

_____

Do you know someone who fits the above description? Describe the rejection that person experienced and the consequences of this response.

_____

_____

People who give in to the system's false judgment can only look forward to more and more rejection. They have bought the lie and even reject themselves.

• **Rebel Against the System**—Rebels and dropouts respond to rejection by saying, "I don't need you or your love." Deep inside they still crave acceptance, but they refuse to acknowledge their need. Full of self-hatred and bitterness, rebels see God as just another tyrant and rebel against Him just like they rebel against everyone else.

What is appealing and even understandable about this response to rejection?

_____

_____

_____

Do you know someone who fits the above description? Describe the rejection that person experienced and the consequences of this response.

_____

_____

_____

This person's rebellious attitude and behavior tend to alienate others, and so the rebel experiences further rejection.

• **Your Response**

Where do you see yourself or traits of yourself in these profiles of negative responses to rejection? Is your approach to beat the system, give in to the system, or rebel against the system? Explain, if you can, why you have chosen that option and the consequences of your choice.

_____

_____

• **Defensiveness Is Defenseless**—There are two reasons why you never need to respond defensively to the world's critical, negative evaluation of you.

First, if you are wrong, you don't *have* a defense. When you're wrong, any defense would be rationalization at best and a lie at worst. Think about times you've been wrong and responded defensively. Was your response a rationalization or a lie?

_____

_____

_____

Why is it so hard to admit when you're wrong instead of being defensive?

_____

_____

_____

Second, if you are right, you don't *need* a defense. The Righteous Judge, who did not revile when He was reviled or make threats when He suffered (see 1 Pet. 2:23), will exonerate you. Comment on that fact. How can this truth make a practical difference in your life?

_____

_____

_____

What did you learn from Neil's conversation with Alice (see pages 215-216)?

_____

_____

_____

As Neil's response to Alice's criticism vividly illustrates, you are not obligated to respond to criticism defensively. After all, the world's system for determining your value as a person is not what determines your value. You are in the world, but you are not of the world. You are in Christ. So if you find yourself responding to rejection defensively, let it remind you to focus your attention on those things that will build up and establish your faith.

DATE:_____

WHEN YOU ARE TEMPTED TO CRITICIZE OR REJECT OTHERS
(PAGES 217-226)

Rejection is a two-way street: You can receive it and you can give it. We've looked at how to respond when you are criticized and rejected. Let's look now at how to respond to the temptation to criticize and reject others.

• Review the situation of Fred and Sue (see pages 217-219).

What does it mean to you that you are responsible for your own character?

_____

_____

What does it mean that you are responsible to meet other people's needs in the context of marriage or any other relationship between believers?

_____

_____

_____

• Relationships don't work when, instead of assuming responsibility for your own character, you attack the other person's character and, instead of looking out for that person's needs, you are selfishly absorbed in meeting your own needs.

Think about the last time you clashed with your spouse, a friend, a coworker or even one of your children. Does the description you just read apply to what was going on? Be specific about how you failed to assume responsibility for your own character and attacked the other person and how you were concerned about your own needs rather than the other person's. An apology and request for forgiveness may be in order.

_____

_____

_____

Answer this somewhat rhetorical question: What kind of families and churches would we have if we all assumed responsibility for our own character and sought to meet the needs of those with whom we live and worship?

_____

_____

_____

Instead of devoting ourselves to developing our own character and to meeting each other's needs, we often yield to Satan's prodding to criticize each other and selfishly consider only ourselves.

• **Focus on Responsibilities**—Another way Satan has deceived us in our interpersonal relationships is by tempting us to focus on our rights instead of our responsibilities.

Describe things you feel you have a right to and therefore tend to demand. (The text gives examples on page 219.)

_____

_____

_____

Now consider the flip side of those rights—your responsibility in the given situation, be it your marriage, your family, your job. (Again, see pages 219-220 of the text.)

_____

_____

_____

What does this discussion about rights versus responsibilities show you about yourself and where you need to be working to become more the person God wants you to be?

_____

_____

What specific step will you take?

_____

_____

When we stand before Christ, He will not ask if we received everything we had coming to us. Instead, He will reward us for how well we fulfilled our responsibilities.

• **Don't Play the Role of Conscience**—Sometimes we are tempted to play the role of the Holy Spirit or conscience in someone else's life.

> How do you respond when someone assumes the role of Holy Spirit or conscience for you? Why do you respond that way?
>
> _____
>
> _____
>
> When have you acted as Holy Spirit or conscience for someone? Be specific about the issue, the person and that person's reaction.
>
> _____
>
> _____
>
> What good came from your self-appointed role as Holy Spirit or conscience? Take note!
>
> _____
>
> _____

The Holy Spirit knows exactly when and how to bring conviction to a person—that's His job. Your job is to surround people with acceptance and love.

• **Discipline Yes, Judgment No**—But there are times when Christians are called to confront their fellow believers. When someone has clearly violated the boundaries of Scripture, we are to accept the sinner but not the sin. We are to confront that person in an attempt to restore him or her to fellowship with God and His people, and Scripture outlines how such church discipline should be handled (see Matt. 18:15,16).

> When have you seen or been a part of the process of church discipline that Jesus describes in Matthew 18:15,16? Describe the process—how easy or difficult it was—and about what happened in the person's life as a result of biblical discipline.
>
> _____
>
> _____

• Be aware that discipline is an issue of confronting behavior you have personally witnessed, but judgment is an issue of character. Disciplining behavior is our job; judging character is God's job.

> With your choice of words, you can too easily cross the line from discipline to character assassination. For instance, rather than calling your son a liar (which is a brutal attack on his character), you say, "Son, you just told a lie," a statement that holds him accountable for observed behavior. Think about what you've said when you discovered someone doing something wrong recently. Where have you crossed the line from discipline to judgment? Give a specific example. Again, an apology and request for forgiveness may be in order.

We must hold people accountable for their behavior, but we are never allowed to denigrate their character.

• **Express Your Needs Without Judging**—If you have legitimate needs in a relationship that are not being met, you are to express those needs in such a way that you don't impugn the other person's character.

> "You don't love me anymore" has a very different impact than "I don't feel loved anymore." How would you react to each of these two statements? Why would you be more receptive to one than the other?

• The nonjudgmental approach of an "I" statement frees the other person to respond to your need instead of defending him- or herself against your attack.

> Do you have trouble asking for your needs to be met? To help you understand the importance of doing so, explain in your own words how *not* expressing your needs can give Satan a foothold in your life.

• When you deny fellow believers the privilege of meeting your needs, you are acting independently of God and leaving yourself vulnerable to the world, the flesh and the devil.

How did you react to the poem on page 225? What points support the truths you've been working with in this lesson?

_____

_____

_____

Anybody can find character defects and performance flaws in another Christian. It takes the grace of God to look beyond people's less-than-saintly behavior to recognize that they are saints in God's eyes. May God give us that grace.

DATE: _____

LIVING WHAT YOU LEARN

A good first step in applying the many truths of this lesson is to focus on making "I" statements rather than "you" statements when you are expressing your needs. Perhaps there is a recurring situation or two for which you can plan an appropriate "I" statement. Also, talk with your spouse and your children about how to express needs without hurting people. Make this a group effort toward eliminating people feeling criticized and rejected in your home.

A WORD OF PRAYER

Lord Jesus, You know what it feels like to be rejected. You know what I have experienced and how I feel inside. Forgive me for responding so differently than You did. Forgive me for trying to beat the system by controlling, manipulating, using and hurting people. Or, for giving in to the system and believing Satan's lies. Or, for being filled with self-hatred and bitterness, rebelling against the system and against You. Forgive me, too, for finding it hard to trust You to judge those who have rejected me. Help me believe that I don't need to respond to criticism and rejection. Help me to trust You to be my defense.

Then, Lord, there's my criticism of others. Forgive me for such unloving ways. Help me to work on developing my own character rather than attacking someone else's, on meeting another's needs rather than seeking to have my needs met, and on fulfilling my God-given responsibilities in various situations rather than demanding my rights. And help me to control my tongue so that I speak words of discipline, not harsh words of judgment and offer "I" messages rather than "you" messages when I share my needs.

God, give me the grace to forgive those who have rejected and hurt me and the grace to love and accept those whom I am tempted to criticize and reject. I pray in Jesus' name, amen.

LOOKING AHEAD

For 12 chapters you've studied growth and what can block it. As this study closes, you'll look at one thing that fosters growth like nothing else does—and that's community.

People Grow Better Together

Y OU'VE LOOKED AT SOME OF THE FACTORS IN YOUR life that can prevent your spiritual growth. You'll end this call to victory over the darkness by looking at a factor that contributes greatly to your spiritual and personal growth: the community of Christ.

DATE:_____

PEOPLE GROW BETTER TOGETHER

(PAGES 227-228)

• Danny had gone to the retreat to learn, not to relate. He wanted content, not community. After two weeks, however, he came to see that spiritual growth and maturity happen best in a community of people who know and accept each other.

How did you learn the truth that "people grow better together"? Describe an experience that made that lesson very clear to you.

_____

_____

_____

Maybe you haven't yet experienced the truth that people grow better together. What do you think about that possibility? If you are skeptical, what will you do to find out whether what was true for Danny will be true for you?

_____

_____

Jesus calls His people to share their lives, not just information about Him, with another. That is the secret to successful discipleship and to spiritual growth.

DATE: _____

RELATIONSHIP: THE HEARTBEAT OF GROWTH AND MATURITY
(PAGES 228-232)

• In a ministry of discipleship, your curriculum must be the Bible and your program must be relationship. Otherwise, you're not doing discipleship. Lots of Bible-based books can be found, but few are the people who will commit themselves to another person so that they can share what Christ is doing in their lives and help each other grow in Him.

When has someone made the commitment to disciple you? Describe the experience you two shared and how you grew spiritually and personally.

_____

_____

_____

When have you made the commitment to disciple another person? Again, describe the experience and how you both grew spiritually and personally.

_____

_____

_____

_____

Discipleship is the intensely personal activity of two or more persons helping each other experience a growing relationship with God, and Jesus modeled this with His twelve disciples. In discipleship, being is before doing, maturity before ministry and character before career.

• Earlier questions asked about formal disciple/discipler relationships in your life. Whatever experiences your answers reflected, know that as a Christian you are both a disciple and a discipler, a learner and a teacher in your Christian relationships.

What role do you have in your family, church or Christian community that gives you the specific responsibility of discipling (teaching) others about God?

_____

_____

What opportunities do you have in your family, church or Christian community to be discipled?

_____

_____

Even as an appointed discipler, you are never not a disciple who is learning and growing in Christ through your relationships. Likewise, even if you don't have an "official" responsibility, you are never not a discipler. In committed, caring relationships with your family members, your friends and other believers, you are both teaching and learning about Christ.

• Similarly, in your Christian relationships, you are both a counselor and a counselee. (Discipleship looks to the future to provoke spiritual growth and maturity, and counseling looks to the past to correct problems and strengthen areas of weakness.)

When have brothers and sisters in the Lord offered you much-needed counsel? When have fellow believers given you much-needed support as you've dealt with areas of weakness and/or problems rooted in the past?

_____

_____

_____

When have you been available to someone who needed counsel, prayer or support of some other kind? Describe what that experience taught you, the counselor.

_____

_____

_____

_____

Whether you are a "professional" discipler and/or counselor or simply a growing Christian who is committed to helping others become mature and experience freedom in Christ, let these designs for discipleship and concepts for counseling equip you for a vital and loving ministry.

DATE: _____

DESIGNS FOR DISCIPLESHIP

(PAGES 232-239)

Based on Paul's words in Colossians 2:6-10, the three levels of the ministry of discipling others deal with the issues of identity, maturity and walking in Christ. Each level is dependent on the previous level(s), and the learning at each level must be experienced in five dimensions: spiritual, rational, emotional, volitional and relational. A point of conflict at each of these five dimensions of application indicates how sin, the world, the flesh and the devil interfere in the discipleship process (see chart on pages 230-231).

• **Level I** addresses **identity** and relates to helping people with the foundational issues of establishing and understanding their identity in Christ.

Review the conflicts of Level I (see pages 233-235). Which conflicts were especially challenging for you? How did you come to resolve those conflicts for yourself?

_____

_____

_____

If you are a Level I believer now, welcome to God's family! Know that He wants you to know of His deep love for you and will enable you to work through the conflicts of this stage (and beyond) as you firmly establish your identity in Christ. Which conflicts are you experiencing now? What are you doing to work through them? Who is or could be a discipler for you?

_____

_____

_____

_____

If you are mature in your faith and able to be a discipler, review the five points of responsibility listed on page 235. Which one(s) do you need to be better prepared to do? What will you do to become better prepared?

_____

_____

• **Level II** deals with **maturity** or growing in Christ, which Paul refers to as "being built up in Him" (Col. 2:7).

Review the conflicts of Level II (see pages 235-237). Which conflicts were especially challenging for you? How did you come to resolve those conflicts for yourself?

_____

_____

_____

If you are a Level II believer now, be encouraged during this stage of sanctification. God is at work in you as you grow in Christlikeness. Which conflicts are you experiencing now? What are you doing to work through them? Who is or could be a discipler for you?

_____

_____

_____

If you are mature in your faith and able to be a discipler, review the five points of responsibility listed on pages 236-237. Which one(s) do you need to be better prepared to do? What will you do to become better prepared?

_____

_____

• **Level III** moves to a believer's daily **walk** in Christ. Such living out of the faith in day-to-day life is founded on a solid identity in Christ and enabled by spiritual maturity. As believers affirm their identity in Christ and grow in maturity, they can be further discipled by a challenge to walk daily in consistent Christian behavior. After all, none of us ever graduates from Level III!

Review the conflicts of Level III (see pages 237-239). Which conflicts are especially challenging for you right now? What are you doing to resolve those conflicts and gain victory over Satan, the world and the flesh?

_____

_____

_____

When you are at this level—and you may be here now—you will find yourself being discipled as well as being a discipler to other Level III believers. With which point(s) of conflict do you need to be better prepared in order to help your fellow believers deal with similar points? What will you do to become better prepared?

_____

_____

_____

The effective Christian walk involves the proper exercise of spiritual gifts, talents and intellect in serving others and being a positive witness in the world. These behavioral objectives are only valid for a person who accepts his or her identity and experiences maturity in Christ. Wherever you are on your spiritual journey, you can celebrate what Christ has already done in your life and look forward to what He will be doing.

DATE: _____

CONCEPTS FOR COUNSELING

(PAGES 239-245)

• Are you willing to commit yourself to being the kind of person someone could confide in? A counselor is a person with whom others feel confident sharing the problems of the present as well as the past.

What are your thoughts and feelings about counseling? Are you wary or skeptical? Unsure how to counsel or if God uses counseling? Confident that one way God heals is through counseling?

_____

_____

_____

Through Christian counselors in a formal arrangement or informal setting, God Himself, the Wonderful Counselor, helps people deal with the present by resolving conflicts from the past. As a Christian and whether or not you have a degree, know that God can and will use you to minister. Here are five practical tips to help you minister to others.

• **Help People Identify Root Issues**—The first goal in counseling is to help the counselee identify the root cause for an unfruitful Christian walk.

> Turn to Figure 13-B on page 241. When have any of the root causes of a barren life interfered with your Christian walk? What did you do about those blocks?
>
> _____
>
> _____
>
> _____
>
> _____
>
> Role-play a counselee dealing with a specific problem of your choosing. What might that person be saying about the situation (a job loss, a broken relationship, trouble with teenage children, etc.) that would help you determine how he or she is doing emotionally, rationally, volitionally, relationally and spiritually? See your listening cues on pages 242-243.
>
> _____
>
> _____
>
> _____

A good counselor knows how to listen to what a counselee is saying—and to what is in between and behind those words.

• **Encourage Emotional Honesty**—Counselees are generally willing to talk about what has happened to them, but they are less willing to admit responsibility and reveal how they feel about the situation. Emotional openness and honesty are key to healing, though. Remember that you cannot be right with God and not be real emotionally.

> Why are people so reluctant to talk about their feelings?
>
> _____
>
> _____

Why have you been or are you reluctant to talk about your feelings?

_____

_____

When have your feelings been a foothold for Satan? Describe what happened when you finally opened up and talked honestly about those feelings.

_____

_____

When Christians in an established relationship keep their emotions in the dark by not sharing them honestly, they give Satan, the prince of darkness, a foothold. Emotional honesty—bringing emotions to light—keeps the devil on the run.

• **Share the Truth**—Life's hard blows can lead many Christians to wonder what's wrong with them. Their perception of God has been distorted, and they feel that He can't possibly love them.

When have hard times made you wonder whether God loves you? What did you do to come to terms with those feelings and to come face–to–face with the truth that He loves you unconditionally and always?

_____

_____

_____

What would you say to someone doubting God's love in the face of life's pain and disappointments? (See "Who Am I?" on pages 45-47 and "Since I Am in Christ" on pages 57-59.) Speak that truth to yourself if you're still trying to accept God's love for you.

_____

_____

What a privilege to share with people, who are hurting, their identity in Christ and to help them adjust their faulty belief system! Once they affirm the truth of their identity in Christ, they can resolve the spiritual, rational, emotional, volitional and relational blocks to their spiritual growth.

• **Call for a Response**—Your role in counseling is to share the truth in love and pray that the counselee will choose to accept it. You cannot choose for him or her.

> What role has prayer played when you have been a counselee (formally or informally)?

_____

_____

_____

_____

> The desired response in counseling is repentance, which means a changing of the mind. What struggles have you had to repent of, first changing your mind and then your ways? Describe one time and let it remind you of what your counselees may be feeling.

_____

_____

_____

Counselees need to change their minds about what they believe about God and themselves. Only then can they change their walk of faith.

• **Help Them Plan for the Future**—First, help your counselees develop a support system of relationships (family, friends, church) and, second, remind them that change takes time.

> How has a strong support system helped you stand strong when life was tough? Describe the support system and list specific kinds of help you received from those involved.

_____

_____

_____

> How have you dealt with the never-fast-enough process of healing and change? What lessons that you learned along the way can you use to counsel and encourage a fellow believer?

_____

_____

The goal of counseling is to help people experience freedom in Christ so that they can move on to maturity and fruitfulness in their walk in Him.

DATE: _____

LIVING WHAT YOU LEARN

If you have begun your spiritual journey relatively recently, pray for someone to disciple you. While you wait for that formal one-on-one relationship with a discipler, begin to work through a Bible-based study of spiritual growth on your own. Also, find a Bible study and experience the joy of Christian community as you learn more about your Lord and Savior and His love.

If you are farther along on your journey, ask God to help you be sensitive to His calling to come alongside someone and disciple him or her in a formal way that will mean mutual growth. In preparation for that discipling, work on those points of conflict (which you identified earlier) where you see yourself as weak.

A Word of Prayer

Gracious and loving God, thank You for being a personal
God—for sending Your Son who died for *my* sins, who is *my*
Savior, and who longs to have a personal relationship with
me. And thank You that I can learn more about You and Your
love in relationships with Your people. Thank You for
putting in my life people to disciple and counsel me. Use me,
Lord, to be a discipler and counselor for my brothers and sisters. I pray in Jesus' name, amen.

Looking Ahead

You are what you are by the grace of God. All you have and can hope for
(as a discipler and disciple, as a counselor and counselee) is based on who
you are in Christ. May your life and your ministry be shaped by your
devotion to Him and the conviction that He is the way, the truth and the
life (see John 14:6). And may God grant you the privilege of seeing people released from the darkness and matured in the light.

Freedom in Christ Ministries

Purpose: Freedom in Christ Ministries is an interdenominational, international, Bible-teaching Church ministry which exists to glorify God by equipping churches and mission groups, enabling them to fulfill their mission of establishing people free in Christ.

Freedom in Christ Ministries offers a number of valuable video, audio, and print resources that will help both those in need and those who counsel. Among the topics covered are:

Resolving Personal Conflicts
Search for Identity ■ Walking by Faith ■ Faith Renewal ■ Renewing the Mind ■ Battle for the Mind ■ Emotions ■ Relationships ■ Forgiveness

Resolving Spiritual Conflicts
Position of Believer ■ Authority ■ Protection ■ Vulnerability ■ Temptation ■ Accusation ■ Deception and Discernment Steps to Freedom

Spiritual Conflicts and Biblical Counseling
Biblical Integration ■ Theological Basis ■ Walking by the Spirit ■ Surviving the Crisis ■ The Process of Growth ■ Counseling and Christ ■ Counseling the Spiritually Afflicted ■ Ritual Abuse

The Seduction of Our Children
God's Answer ■ Identity and Self-Worth ■ Styles of Communication ■ Discipline ■ Spiritual Conflicts and Prayer ■ Steps to Freedom

Resolving Spiritual Conflicts and Cross-Cultural Ministry
Dr. Timothy Warner
Worldview Problems ■ Warfare Relationships ■ Christians and Demons ■ The Missionary Under Attack ■ Practical Application for Missionaries ■ Steps to Freedom in Christ

For additional resources from Dr. Anderson's ministry write or call us at:

Freedom in Christ Ministries
491 E. Lambert Road, La Habra, California 90631
Phone: (310) 691-9128 ■ Fax: (310) 691-4035

*More books from Neil Anderson
to help you and those you love
find freedom in Christ.*

Victory over the Darkness
Regal Books

Victory over the Darkness Study Guide
Regal Books

The Bondage Breaker
Harvest House Publishers

The Bondage Breaker Study Guide
Harvest House Publishers

Spiritual Warfare (Timothy M. Warner)
Crossway Books

Winning Spiritual Warfare
Harvest House Publishers

Walking in the Light
Thomas Nelson Publishers

The Seduction of Our Children
Harvest House Publishers

Released from Bondage
Thomas Nelson Publishers

Breaking Through to Spiritual Maturity
Regal Books

Living Free in Christ
Regal Books

Daily in Christ
Harvest House Publishers

The Bondage Breaker Youth Edition
Harvest House Publishers

The Slimeball Memos (Richard Miller)
Harvest House Publishers

Stomping Out the Darkness
Regal Books

Setting Your Church Free
Regal Books

*These and many other helpful resources are available
at your local Christian bookstore.*

Learn to Fight on Your Knees.

There's a battle raging, an unseen struggle in the heavens that affects the way we live as Christians. But how can you fight against a force which can't be seen, an invisible enemy desperate to foil God's plan? The answer is prayer. That's because the battle against Satan has already been won, paid for by the price of Christ's blood. You can discover the truth behind spiritual warfare and what you can do to advance the cause of Christ around the world through these factual, biblical guides from Regal Books.

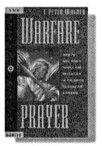

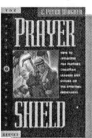

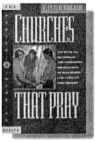

Warfare Prayer
Book One of the "Prayer Warrior" Series
C. Peter Wagner
A biblical and factual guide which will help you seek God's power and protection in the battle to build His kingdom.
ISBN 08307.15347

Prayer Shield
Book Two of the "Prayer Warrior" Series
C. Peter Wagner
Here is a tool to help you teach lay people how to intercede in prayer for your ministry.
ISBN 08307.15738

Breaking Strongholds in Your City
Book Three of the "Prayer Warrior" Series
C. Peter Wagner
Learn how to identify the enemy's territory in your city, along with practical steps to help you pray against these dark strongholds.
ISBN 08307.15975

Churches That Pray
Book Four of the "Prayer Warrior" Series
C. Peter Wagner
Take a comprehensive look at prayer and how new forms of prayer can break down the walls between the church and the community— locally and globally.
ISBN 08307.15983

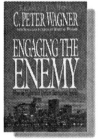

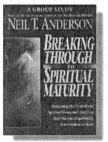

Engaging the Enemy
Edited by
C. Peter Wagner
John Dawson, Peter Wagner and 16 others provide guidance based on their experiences with territorial spirits.
ISBN 08307.15169

Victory over the Darkness
Neil T. Anderson
Dr. Neil Anderson shows that we have the power to conquer the darkness, once we know who we are in Christ.
ISBN 08307.13751

Breaking Through to Spiritual Maturity
Neil T. Anderson
Take possession of the victory Christ freely offers and mature in your faith with this 13- to 24-week course. Based on best-sellers *Victory over the Darkness* and *The Bondage Breaker*.
ISBN 08307.15312

Wrestling with Dark Angels
Compiled by
C. Peter Wagner and F. Douglas Pennoyer
Spiritual warfare is going on all around us. This collection of essays gives readers the understanding they need to fight back.
ISBN 08307.14464

These and all Regal Books are available at your local Christian bookstore.

Regal Books
A Division of Gospel Light